DEAR BIRMINGHAM

DEAR BIRMINGHAM

a conversation with My Hometown

KARAMAT IQBAL

Cover: Lisa Charrington-Wilden
Author photo: Adam Iqbal

This book was printed in the United States of America.

Rev. date: 04/19/2013

To order additional copies of this book, contact:
Xlibris Corporation
0-800-644-6988
www.xlibrispublishing.co.uk
Orders@xlibrispublishing.co.uk
304943

CONTENTS

SECTION 1

SECTION 2

SECTION 3

Dedicated

- To the memory of my father Sufi Mohammed Iqbal, my uncle Chaudhry Mohammed Yaqub and other pioneers from our family and community who laid the foundations for Pakistani-Birmingham

- To my mother and sisters; if only you had had the opportunity to realise your potential

- To the current and future generations of Brummies.

Acknowledgements

- My thanks to Lisa Charrington-Wilden for catching my vision, to Caroline Wilkes for insightful editorial input and to Adam Iqbal for 'that' picture.

- Thank you to my anonymous 'critical friends' for their comment on earlier drafts of this document.

- For her unstinting support, a big 'thank you' to Sue Iqbal; a true woman of courage and foresight!

SECTION 1

DEAR BIRMINGHAM

Thank you for being my home for the past forty plus years. Thank you also for welcoming my father and others in our family and community during the fifties. You as a city welcomed them, us, because you needed their labour and they came willingly because they needed jobs. As we have learnt, it has benefited the city in many ways. It has certainly benefited our community, both here and back in Pakistan. I grew up in a brick house, the first in our village, thanks to the money earned in Birmingham.

But, now, after the 50th anniversary of the Commonwealth Immigration Act 1962 has been and gone a different kind of reception is needed. Let us have the Pakistani community welcomed into the whole of our city; all its nooks and corners. Let us have no 'Pakistanis are not welcome here' signs, visible or invisible, outside any of our organisations, setting out to exclude this large community. I strongly believe that the success of the Pakistani community is intertwined with the success of our great city; which can has the potential for becoming greater still.

In my conversations about Dear Birmingham, without fail, people have raised the question: "but, what about the Pakistani community itself?" Indeed! Has the community done enough to become an integral part of the society here? During the drafting stage, one 'critical friend' pointed out:

> *"While the British Pakistani culture has many admirable strengths, are there any areas which might need addressing / developing to face the Western world of the 21st century, especially its employment needs?*

How might Pakistani boys be encouraged from within the community, as well as within the wider society of which they're a part? Where are the really good role models in the British Pakistani community and how might they be deployed more effectively to inspire a new generation?

What role might the mosque play in raising aspiration? What kind of multiculturalism should we aim at as a whole society?"

In a message to his fellow Pakistanis, *Quiad e Azam*, the great leader, Mohammed Ali Jinnah had once said: "The more you organise yourself, the more you will be able to get your rights." As we have learnt from history, they heard him and did achieve their rights, more than even they could imagine then. This was on 24 March 1940, the day after that famous gathering in Lahore which had resolved to fight for the new country of Pakistan.

Given the community's size and potential in Birmingham, who knows what it may be able to achieve if it were to organise itself and put its resources to good use. On another occasion, addressing young people, Mr Jinnah had said: "Education is a matter of life and death for us." This has never been truer than now in Birmingham when so many of Pakistani young people leave school without the qualifications they need to get on in life.

For more recent advice to the community, I turn to Dr Maliha Lodhi. For five years, she was Pakistani High Commissioner to the UK. In an interview, while acknowledging the dynamic nature of the Pakistani community, she said it was possible to become an integral member of British society without being totally assimilated. For her, this was the only way of beating the extremists within the Pakistani community and racists outside of it, both of whom wish to do harm to the community and its relations with the wider world. Referring to the community's media characterisations, she advised: "Stand up. Don't let others define you or mis-define you."[1]

I have not suggested which organisation should do what. For me, Dear Birmingham is aimed at the whole of the city community. Depending on who you are and your purpose, you can decide for yourself the implications the document has for you. This includes the many organisations in the private, public and third sectors which I have not been able to investigate. All of what has been written applies equally to them, as employers and service providers.

A meeting of Pakistani religious leaders, held recently at Faiz-ul-Quran in Alum Rock concluded that they alone could not tackle the problems facing their community; it required a joined-up strategy involving political, social and religious organisations.[2] Much of what they were discussing has resulted from a system-failure and the solutions will equally be found with everyone working together.

We all need to play our full role. Otherwise the picture could be very bleak. If over a hundred thousand Brummies do not come in from the cold of the inner city into the warm welcome of the wider community and help build our collective future then that is a prospect none of us would wish for. I look forward to the day when my community of birth is fully integrated into the life of My Hometown.

So Dear Birmingham, Pakistanis and the rest, it is upto us to decide what kind of city we wish to leave for future generations. I hope we, all of us together, will attend to the issues raised in this letter.

Karamat Iqbal
-   a concerned Brummy.

INTRODUCTION

We have come to take equality for granted. For David Goodhart, the subject has even become banal.[3] We certainly have laws in place which demand that we do not practice unfair discrimination. Organisations have policies and, sometimes, detailed guidance which tell their staff what to do and we collect more data than we know what do with. So, what is there to worry about? For the answer, we have to look a little closer.

For much of my adult life, I have been active in the promotion of equality. This began with a focus on Pakistanis and slowly broadened to include other ethnic and social groups. As time has gone on, I have seen more and more organisations make claims, in a taken-for-granted fashion, that equality has been achieved. However, often the claims conflicted with what I saw in relation to the local Pakistani community. For some reason, they still seemed to be waiting for the opportunities and benefits which other groups could take for granted. Not one to rely on simple anecdotal evidence, I decided to investigate the situation in a more systematic way.

I am aware that, compared to many towns and cities, we as a city have done well. For example, we have made a successful transition in the area of employment so now it is possible to make a respectable living without getting one's hands dirty. I had also become used to reading the kind of comment as this one:

> *"Great cities recognise cultural diversity as a real strength. It is the collective harmony of Birmingham people working together which makes it an exciting place to live and work. If we are divided we will not be able to take advantage of the opportunities of the new century."*—Councillor Sir Albert Bore (Evening Mail, 3 May 2000)

I wondered, however, whether this was true for everyone. Did it also apply to the Pakistani community; did they also benefit from the riches of our 'great city'? I then came across a comment from Tahir Abbas pointing out that while Birmingham had been a success overall, minorities like the Pakistanis (he had said Muslims) had not had a share in that success. Professor Abbas, a rarity as a Pakistani academic, is a son of the city and has a particularly insightful perspective on our community. Educated in our schools, he was at the time the head of the Centre for Ethnicity and Culture at Birmingham University. He is currently based at the University of Istanbul.

Abbas had pointed out that with the decline of its manufacturing and engineering sectors the city had undergone regeneration by expanding into the service sectors. But these opportunities had "largely evaded most Muslims and they may have even entrenched some of the barriers" faced by them. He stated that "one in six working Pakistani men in Britain is a taxi driver is indicative for the labour exclusions faced." Moreover, he pointed out that in Birmingham "Muslims appear to have been neglected by the state and 'third way' public services" i.e. the third sector:

> "The city's Pakistanis are often excluded from this experience of change and development because of structural subordination and existing conditions of exclusion, racism, poverty, other disadvantages, and limited political impact, which is perennially constrained by internal divisions and external challenges."

Elsewhere in the same article he has pointed out that:

> "Pakistanis experience high rates of unemployment, high rates of underachievement in education, higher rates of imprisonment, poorer health and some of the worst housing."[4],

This seemed a damning comment on the place I call My Hometown (after Bruce Springsteen). Was there some truth in this comment, I wondered? I began to investigate the matter.

After a number of conversations with trusted colleagues, the first formal meeting I had was at Birmingham Chamber on 22 November 2010. I was directed to the Pakistan High Commission who put me in touch with their Consul General in Birmingham. After meeting him the following February, I went to see my local MP.

The next key meeting was with one of the City Council's Directors who referred me to their Equalities Department, Dr Mashuq Ally. He informed me that it was unlikely that anyone would fund what I wished to do because "all have done their own research" though he did say that no one was joining it up; "things are done in silos."

From then on the challenge for me was clear and clearly stated. My job was to try to persuade whoever would listen that Pakistanis in Birmingham should be seen as everyone's responsibility and not just an 'equalities' matter. Pakistanis are here in such large numbers that we should surely treat them as a mainstream matter.

My journey continued. Dr Ally had referred me to the Pakistani Community Development Network (hereinafter Pakistani Network)[5]. Led by a dedicated group who give their time for free to serve the needs of their community, it is one of eleven such networks which exist within Birmingham to represent the views of different communities and is led by a dedicated group who give their time for free to serve the needs of their community.[6]

I visited Pakistani Network website[7] and found a number of statements which for them summed up the situation facing Birmingham's Pakistani community. For example:

> *"Poverty and unemployment continue to impact far more heavily on the community. Many Pakistanis are self-employed in the taxi business, takeaways and retail businesses. The public sector has largely failed to employ members of the community."*

The Pakistani Network were supportive of my desire to write a report on Pakistani-Birmingham and made a funding application to help me undertake the research. Although, they did not succeed in this, their support in-kind was worth more than any money they could raise. After this I did not need any further encouragement to write this note to the city and all who live and work in it in the hope they are equally concerned for its future.

STRUCTURE OF THE DOCUMENT

The document is made up of four sections. Section one starts with my letter to 'My Hometown' and details of my connection with the city. It is necessary to point out here that some of my story is also the story of Pakistani-Birmingham. I provide a note about my recent inspiration for this social commentary and a list of key texts which, between them provide a background to the development of our diverse community.

In section two, I outline the development of the Pakistani community in the city, the good, bad and the ugly too. I offer the community's current position in the city, making a case that the issues raised should be treated as a mainstream matter. Here, I provide population statistics, employment data generally and with a particular focus on the City Council and other public sector organisations. I provide data from the world of education, health and criminal justice services; in terms of Pakistani service users, employees and the participation by the community in the decision making structures of the institutions concerned. Some data from the private sector is also provided. However, this is restricted to those employers who are delivering public sector contracts. I focus on the extent to which Pakistanis are included in the city's 'picture' by considering the coverage given to the community by the Birmingham Mail over a four-week period.

In section three, I provide my conclusions and some comment on what I believe the problem to be. I question the 'myth of merit' and suggest that there might be at play, in our city, particular types of racisms affecting the Pakistani community. I suggest that there is more to parallel living than generally accepted and suggest ways of 'wiping the slate clean' in order to create a 'we' city. I engage in an honest conversation with a 'son' of the city. I also talk about how Pakistanis are different from other communities and suggest that 'treating them the same' is perhaps not the answer. I focus on the controversial area of religion and suggest that it should be given more space in our public square, schools and other organisations as the 'religious' amongst us increase in number. It is suggested that we should review our alcohol-based culture and the lack of halal food in our city centre restaurants given their implications, good and bad, for cohesion. Given that nearly a half of our city community is made up of 'minorities', I wonder whether it is time we encouraged greater bilingualism amongst our citizens. I then offer some concluding thoughts.

Finally, in section four, I provide ideas for possible action if we wish for a different future for the city. This includes a list of what I have called 'Birmingham Principles'. Just as I started I finish with a Dear Birmingham note, except this one invites the readers to respond with their thoughts and ideas.

Note: Much of the data I present here was obtained through Freedom of Information 2000 requests, submitted *www.WhatDoTheyKnow.com* which had been set up by Chris Lightfoot. It is by far the easiest way of gathering such information.

BACKGROUND TO MY RELATIONSHIP WITH BIRMINGHAM

I arrived in Birmingham in 1970, at age 12, from Dadyal, District Mirpur, Azad Kashmir. After spending two terms at Steward Reception Centre, I transferred to Nechells Secondary School. I left here at age 16. I was, what they referred to in those days as, a 'ROSLA' kid so that extra year resulting from the raising of the school leaving age for me made a great deal of difference.

During the 1950s, people from our community were arriving in Birmingham. One of my uncles was a pioneer. Having fought for the British in Burma during World War II, he decided he would help to rebuild Britain, and make a bit of money too. So he came and settled here. Soon after, he was able to buy a house, in Nechells.

At the time newcomers to the city had to be here for five years before they could even join the council house waiting list. Furthermore, when it came to buying property, estate agents, building societies and individuals who were selling houses could racially discriminate if they wanted to and some did. Most of the men from our family, who came to England, were to start their life in Britain at my uncle's house. This included my own father who lived there from 1957 to 1962. I too spent my first few years there before moving to other parts of the city.

At school, I was a conscientious student. The culture I had come from had taught me to value education and respect my teachers as my spiritual parents. While still going through my compulsory education, I had signed up to evening classes at the nearby Duddeston Adult Education Institute. I also made good use of my local, Bloomsbury, library.

Upon leaving school, I began work at British Steel Corporation in Bromford and was given day-release to continue my education, at Sutton Coldfield FE College. I also continued with my evening classes. Wanting to make a difference to the world around me, in any spare time I had, I became active in the Asian Youth Association which had been set up by the Birmingham Community Relations Council. We organised a cultural evening to raise the awareness of my, mainly White, factory colleagues.

I lived near Saltley Community Development Project. With encouragement from its Editor, Sultan Mahmood Hashmi, I began to write for their bilingual community newspaper. I also helped out at education and leisure activities at Norton Hall. It was here that I saw David Edgar's play, Destiny, being performed. This was about trade unions, equality and justice. Of particular interest to me was the fact that one of the actors was the Pakistani Tariq Younis. I also became active in Saltley Asian Action Group which had been set up in response to racist activity of the National Front. I recall attending a meeting with Jagmohan Joshi, the founding leader of the Indian Workers Association.

At the age of 20, I became an employee of the City Council, in the role of Trainee Youth Worker. These posts had been created as 'Positive Action' to recruit unqualified minority ethnic staff and to give them an opportunity to gain qualifications and training. Of the eight posts, two of us were Asian; the rest were from the Caribbean community. I was based at the community centre in Muntz Street and then at the Naseby Centre in Alum Rock. During the second year, I was given the opportunity to do a short placement at the Mere Green Youth Club. I was keen to work with a mainly White community. It was generally a positive experience with the exception of the occasional racist abuse from the young people I worked with.

As well as helping to establish some of the early youth provision for Asian young people in the city, I organised events targeted specifically at the Pakistani community. This included a day-long programme on 23 March, to mark Pakistan Day. I also initiated, as an evening class, the 10-week Asian Studies course. This provided training in multicultural issues for teachers, probation officers and other public sector professionals. The course had input from community activists such as Avtar Johal, Tony Huq and Ranjit Sondhi.

While working as a Youth Worker, I also organised a few *kabaddi* competitions; one at Small Heath Park and another at Salford Stadium. This was to provide opportunities for fun for our community as well as to bridge-build between Pakistanis and Indians whose teams competed against each other.

I was given time off to study sociology at Mathew Boulton College. It was during this period that I discovered books such as *A portrait of English racism* and *Because they're black;* the latter had won the Martin Luther King Memorial prize in 1972. It was through these seminal works that I learnt about the treatment of my community in the early days, when my father was here. I learnt about a phenomenon called 'Paki-bashing'. One book had a whole chapter on the subject.[8]

I also learnt the early history[9] of Pakistanis in Birmingham. When Dr Anwar published his ground breaking book about Pakistanis, pointing out that they were here to stay[10], I was to join him in a discussion on the local Radio WM.

At the end of the youth work job, I attended Westhill College. Upon qualifying as a teacher I worked for the then Birmingham Multicultural Support Service, teaching English to newly arrived pupils.

I then spent the next 15 years in Wolverhampton; at Race Equality Council and then Bilston Community College. I was able to develop my knowledge and skills through my involvement in some cutting-edge practice. I also appreciated the opportunity to work with African Caribbean, Indian and White working class communities.

During this period, I achieved my Masters from Birmingham University, in Race and Education. Much of my teaching took place in the Centre for Contemporary Cultural Studies, made famous by its leader Professor Stuart Hall.

Upon leaving my job at Bilston, in 2000, we set up the Forward Partnership consultancy, named in part after the City's motto. Through this and as an associate of other, larger, organisations, I have had the opportunity to undertake a number of quite prestigious national assignments.

Parallel with the above role, I worked as a part-time Education Adviser, based within the Birmingham Advisory and Support Service. Here, I worked on educational underachievement, especially of White working class pupils. I produced a number of research reports which I was able to use in 'championing' this unrepresented community. My work was used as the main source for a parliamentary debate on White underachievement—instigated by Richard Burden, MP for Birmingham Northfield[11]. According to a Google search of 'Hansard White achievement', this would appear to be one of the few recent debates on the subject. Hopefully, one day I will be in a position to do the same for Pakistani pupils.

Having been there at the start of the City's developments in multi-cultural and anti-racist education in the 1980s, sadly, now I was observing some of the colour-blind approaches that were being taken in education. Instead of taking a differentiated approach, now there was a belief that "a good school is a good school regardless . . ." and "if it works with one underachieving group, it will work with another." The pioneering groups, set up by Professor Sir Tim Brighouse, to address underachievement were being abandoned. Fortunately, by the time I left my job, I had laid the foundations for Dear Birmingham and my current doctoral research on Pakistani boys' education.

07/05/21

A note about my inspiration for Dear Birmingham

> The intellectual's job is to tell people how reality really is—to look it in the face
>
> —Stuart Hall

> The duty of the intellectual is to denounce injustice wherever it occurs
>
> —Jean-Paul Sartre

> "Knowledge' is not a goal in itself, but a path to wisdom; it bestows not privilege so much as duty, not power so much as responsibility."
>
> —Sivanandan

I have drawn on ideas from individuals of many backgrounds following the advice of Abu Yusef Al-Kindi who lived 801-873 AD. As well as a philosopher, I am told that he was a scientist of high caliber, a gifted mathematician, astronomer, physician and a geographer as well as a talented musician. He said:

> "We ought not to be embarrassed of appreciating the truth and of obtaining it wherever it comes from, even if it comes from races distant and nations different from us. Nothing should be dearer to the seeker of truth than the truth itself, and there is no deterioration of the truth, nor belittling either of one who speaks it or conveys it."

While I have been working on 'Dear Birmingham' there have been a few books which have helped to shape my thinking. Top of the list is 'Orientalism' by Edward Said which has absolutely transformed my worldview.

Another book that has similarly influenced me is Stanley Wolpert's 'Jinnah of Pakistan'. I wished to understand the founder of Pakistan. How is it that a person who we Pakistanis refer to as, *Quaid e Azam*, Great Leader, could be portrayed so negatively in the West! The book has answered some of my questions. It has also raised my self-esteem manifold; to read about such giant of a man coming from the same world as I. Whenever I feel the need to uplift myself in relation to my Pakistani identity, I just have to read the following opening sentences from the book:

> *"Few individuals significantly alter the course of history. Fewer still modify the map of the world. Hardly anyone can be credited with creating a nation-state. Mohammed Ali Jinnah did all three"*

My generation owes a debt to two particular early campaigners for equality for immigrants: Dhani Prem, an Indian doctor who came to Birmingham in 1939 and Henry Gunter[12], a Jamaican who had migrated here in 1949. Prem served on the Executive Committee of Birmingham Labour Party and for several years as a City Councillor.

Gunter had skills in accountancy, but the only job he could get was in a brass rolling mill in Deritend. According to Sutcliffe & Smith "some firms which employed coloured people in the works were said to be reluctant to take them into the office." Given that he was very keen to help improve things for Black workers who faced a great deal of hostility, Gunter became active in the trade union movement. As a representative of his union, AUEW, he was to be selected as a member of the Birmingham Trades Council, the first ever Black person to do so.

Gunter became known for his campaigns against racism which privileged the mainstream White community at the expense of his own and other minorities such as the Pakistanis. He wrote letters and articles in the local press and, on 12 October 1952, organised a major demonstration against the colour bar. In response to that famous demonstration, Birmingham Trades Council resolved to condemn British colonial policies

Key text

Following are a number of texts I have used as background for Dear Birmingham. When making reference to these documents I shall do so by using the name(s) of the author(s):

- Dummett, Ann: *A portrait of English racism* CARAF, 1973
- Fanon Frantz: *Black skin White masks* Macgibbon & Kee, 1968
- Grosvenor, Ian: *Assimilating Identities* Lawrence and Wishart, 1997
- Gunter, Henry: *A man's a man, a study of colour bar in Birmingham and an answer* 1954
- Howell, Denis: *Made in Birmingham*—the memoirs, Macdonald 1990
- Humphry, Derek and John, Gus: *Because they're black* Pelican 1972
- Newton, Kenneth: *Second City Politics* Birmingham Clarendon Press 1976
- Prem, Dhani: *The Parliamentary Leper—Colour and British Politics* 1965
- Solomos, John and Back, Les: *Race, Politics and Social Change,* Routledge 1995
- Sutcliffe, Anthony and Smith, Roger: *Birmingham 1939-1970,* (especially chapter XI: *The impact of coloured immigration*) Oxford University 1974
- Uglow, Jenny; *The Lunar Men* Faber and Faber 2002

SECTION 2

PAKISTANI-BIRMINGHAM; A MAINSTREAM ISSUE

When Dhani Prem came to Birmingham as a locum tenens in 1939, he spoke of "the dilapidated slum area of Alum Rock and Nechells". In a 1973 report by the local Community Development Project, it was pointed out that while other ethnic groups were keen to move out of Saltley, Pakistanis were happy to move in and set up shop, sometimes literally as the profile of the local businesses was to show. The community were happy to keep themselves to themselves.[13] On another occasion it was reported that as many as 94% of the, mainly Pakistani, Asians, of Balsall Heath were content to go on living in the area[14]. I am not surprised; given that many parts of the city were not welcoming places for them, nor did they have the money to buy more expensive houses elsewhere.

While areas such as Aston, Saltley and Sparkbrook are still the main centres for the community, it would appear that they are on the move towards other parts of the city which previously had few Pakistanis. According to the most recent data from the Council, 20 of the 40 city wards have 10% or more Pakistanis (Annex 1). Even the traditionally White parts of the city have small numbers of the community as their neighbours. Sheldon, Bournville, Oscott, Sutton Vesey and Shard End each have at least 2% Pakistanis. Furthermore, all wards of the city now have more than 1.5% Muslims amongst their community.

A brief history of Pakistani-Birmingham

Having exploited the people of the Empire and won both World Wars with their help, Britain now needed their help with its rebuilding programme after the destruction of World War II. There were plenty of jobs which needed to be done but which its own population did not wish to do—too dirty, too little money! So the 1948 Nationality Act was passed, making the ex-colonials British citizens. They could come and go as they pleased. So they came; first from the Caribbean on the ship *Empire Windrush* and then from the Indian sub-continent, many settling in Birmingham.

At the same time as India gained its independence from the British, a new country, Pakistan, came into being in 1947. One of the areas affected by the Partition was the seriously under-developed state of Kashmir. In what has been described as "impetuous and possibly unprincipled haste" in which the British had left India, the future of this mainly Muslim state was only faced up to in the final few weeks, when "a vigorous though morally questionable attempt was made to dispose of it in tidy and conclusive fashion."[15] As a result of a war between Pakistan and India, Kashmir became divided. One third of it, known as Azad Kashmir, came to be controlled by Pakistan and two-thirds by India. Officially the area is still a disputed territory.

From the stories we were told as children, Azad Kashmir had little to offer its citizens in terms of work. Many people had depended on employment outside the area; in other parts of united India under British rule. After Partition, when they could no longer freely travel to much of the sub-continent, they began to look elsewhere and found Britain as a new 'land of opportunity'. Thus, the foundations for Pakistani-Birmingham came to be laid, with some 80% coming from Azad Kashmir.

The reception in Birmingham!

Birmingham's initial reaction to the post-war Black and Asian settlement had been one of political and social panic. The city had a policy of indirect discrimination against immigrants in housing and its sole gesture towards meeting the needs of immigrants was to appoint a somewhat ill-equipped 'Liaison Officer for Coloured People'. There was some talk (hope?) at the time that the immigrants may one day go back so training in agriculture was organised for them on the assumption that this would be useful for them 'back home'.

The political parties were hostile towards the newcomers. This hostility had a national backdrop. It may be difficult to believe now but people such as Winston Churchill, while appreciating the colonials' war effort, now did not want them in their country as a part of 'Keep England

White' movement to which he belonged. The same slogan was used by the supporters of the fascist leader Oswald Mosley, when they marched in the late 1950s through Sparkbrook. Harry Watton, the leader of the Labour group on the Council, is quoted, by Grosvenor, as making a distinction between White Brummies and Black people: "Birmingham people must come first—that is where I stand personally and that is where I hope the Labour Group will stand."

Soon after the 1959 general election a group of Tory MPs from the Birmingham area launched a systematic campaign for the introduction of immigration controls. A lobbying organisation, the Birmingham Immigration Control Association, was set up. The first Commonwealth Immigrants Bill, described by the Labour leader Hugh Gaitskell as 'miserable, shameful, shabby' became law in 1962. "This was to be the first legislation passed purely for racist reasons."[16] Although, its impact was to restrict the entry of both Black and Asian people, one politician is on record for saying that the legislation was purely to keep Asians out. This was followed by another racist law, towards the end of the decade. This time, its purpose was to keep British passport holding Asians from East Africa out of the country. It took about three days for Parliament to put the legislation on the statute books.

Prem talked of discrimination faced by immigrants. He spoke of trade union pressure to deny them certain jobs. For example, when immigrants applied for jobs as bus conductors, the Secretary of the Transport & General Workers Union objected on the grounds that "the white women members of the bus-crew would not be safe and their parents would never permit them to work with coloured workers." Elsewhere, Prem explains that "when the Birmingham busmen objected to coloured colleagues in 1954, it was not because these would be taking jobs which might otherwise have gone to Birmingham lads but because it was feared they might have an effect on wages which a shortage of labour had maintained at an artificial level."

Elsewhere, Prem has spoken of the discrimination faced by the professionals in the immigrant community:

> "One of the City hospitals had a vacancy. A West Indian doctor from Edinburgh University, with an imposing English name, applied. On the strength of his qualifications and testimonials he was given the job, without the preliminaries of an interview.

The doctor duly arrived. There was a commotion. The medical staff telephoned the Chairman of the Hospital's Committee.

"Surely there is some mistake", said the Chairman.

"No, sir, I do not think so. Here is the letter of appointment."

The Chairman glanced at the letter and said, with an *innocent smile* (my emphasis), "Ah, I thought so". It *is* (original emphasis) a clerical mistake. Two doctors of the same name. I am sorry. We shall offer you an apology, your return fare and one month's salary"

Prem goes on to say: "these are not isolated examples. Many (similar) stories can be told of landladies, works managers, public houses and government services".

Others have pointed out that Black and Asian people were "wanted for their labour but not as neighbours"[17]. This was very true for the situation in Birmingham. A recent article shedding new light on our past has quoted a 'Windrush' Jamaican as saying: "Birmingham people are the most unfriendly I have ever met. There seems to be a great colour bar here." Another immigrant commented: "Our intention in coming to Britain was to find work. We have found work but we have nowhere to live."[18]

According to one survey, sighted by Sutcliffe & Smith, of White people "over 98 per cent said that they would be unwilling to take a coloured lodger." The authors mention how "in May 1948 a crowd of about 200 men besieged and stoned a Birmingham house where Indians were staying." Professor Stuart Hall has spoken of facing signs such as "we don't take any Blacks here', when he moved to Birmingham in 1964.[19]

It was this same environment which had forced people like my father and uncle to make ends meet by living 'cheek by jowl' in inner city Birmingham. They worked shifts in factories and slept shifts in beds.

In terms of public policy towards immigrants in the city, there appeared to be an attitude of 'do nothing'. For Sutcliffe &Smith, it was a colour-blind policy of treating everyone the same even though people had different needs and circumstances.

Prem also spoke of the government doing little in housing, education or recreation for the immigrants. "No efforts were made by local authorities for integration. The result was that the immigrants were left to fend for themselves. They went to those areas where there was work and where friends could provide for them with shelter." This *separate development* meant that the great majority of English people in the city, other than at work, rarely came into contact with the newcomers. While this may have helped to avoid racial conflict, it also gave rise to people leading 'parallel lives'; a concept we were to discover during the later debate on community cohesion.

The following from an article by Professor Sir Tim Brighouse, tells us how immigrants were thought of locally:

> **B**irmingham children are White and they're Black
> **I**mmigrants come, we can't send them back
> **R**eally we'd like to but now they're here
> **M**illions who multiply year after year
> **I**t's our job to teach them to live just like us
> **N**icely and soberly without any fuss
> **G**od knows how we'll do it, we'd all like to try
> **H**ave you desire to give help and try?
> **A**nd teach in our schools? We'll see you get paid
> **M**ay we please employ you to give us your aid? [20]

There was a similar national backdrop. Our own Denis Howell, MP, played quite a central role here, as detailed in his autobiography. The government of the day was very concerned with the arrival of immigrant children in the nation's schools. It didn't want too many of them in any one school. So, it turned to Mr Howell for advice. In his own words, what happened next is very enlightening indeed about making national policy and which was to impact on race relations in a fundamental way:

> *"One of the difficulties was that no one could advise me as to what percentage figure I should put in my proposals to represent the maximum of immigrant children it was desirable to have in any one school or in any one class in a school. There was no professional advice available."*

So, Mr Howell announced one Friday as he was going home to his family in Birmingham, that he would have an answer by Monday morning. He did as promised. On Monday, he announced: "It is to be one third, write it into the circular." This was the famous 'Circular 7/65: *Education of Immigrants*', the first example of national policy in this context. This is how Mr Howell had come to his decision:

> *"What I had done that morning was to call at Park Hill School to ask Mr Labon the question I thought to be paramount: 'How large a percentage of immigrant children do we have now, and what is the maximum percentage of such children that you can take while still being able to guarantee to parents like me that you can maintain the standards of education for our children."*

I wonder who he had in mind when he spoke of 'parents like me' and 'our children'.

> *"My officials appeared incredulous when I explained all this to them but they could not produce any challenge on professional grounds so that was that. I was much reassured some months later when the Birmingham branch of the National Union of Teachers carried out a study, which was also accepted by the NUT nationally, proposing a 30 per cent maximum."* (p188).

It would appear the policy was too late for Birmingham. There were too many schools already with more than 30% immigrant children. It would have been too difficult to arrange transport in order to move them across the city. It was also felt that the White parents in the Outer Ring would not have liked to see immigrant children arriving in their schools. I don't know whether they ever considered moving White children to the Inner Ring schools in order to create a racial balance. So, upset though it made Mr Howell to see his own city going against his policy, things were left as they were. A number of other education authorities did follow the government advice and embarked on their policy of 'bussing' immigrant children to more White areas in order to achieve a racial balance.

But, it wasn't all bad!

It would be unfair to our city if we did not mention some of the 'good' that has also been a part of its later history. The incoming Labour administration, in the 1980s, had made clear its commitment to a multicultural and anti-racist education:

"Curriculum must reflect the diversity of cultures in our society and must positively counter racism"

"Multi-cultural curriculum must apply to all subjects, all age groups and all schools and colleges"

"In-service training for teachers with particular emphasis on training in racism awareness"

"Greater recruitment of ethnic minority teachers."

The policy was then implemented in the local schools through the establishment of the Multicultural Support Service, which contained within it a number of units. One of these was the Multicultural Development Unit which had 34 experienced teachers who were strategically placed in primary and secondary schools. Apart from teaching, their job was to assist in the whole process of moving towards an education that better meets the needs of all pupils in a multicultural city. Another was the Afro-Caribbean Teaching Unit, made up of 7 experienced teachers. There were also the Community Languages Unit and an English as a second language unit which I had joined upon training as a teacher.

The above service produced the Multicultural Review. Each issue carried articles including some written by practising Birmingham teachers. Edited by David Ruddell, it was circulated to all schools, free of charge. Following is a sample of the articles from the journal:

- Michael Hussey explaining multi-racial, multi-cultural, and multi-ethnic;
- A review of the Race Relations teaching pack which had been produced by the Lozells-based organisation, AFFOR (all faiths for one race);
- Helen Butcher on 'racial bias in books: a strategy for action'
- Gay Baldwin and Ray Chatwin asking 'Must it be Urdu versus English?' when discussing bilingualism in the classroom at Bordesely Green Girls school
- The Editor on: 'What role for 'White' schools' with reference to the city's 'Education for a multicultural society' policy
- A feature on the Muslim communities

- Sue Watts on 'science education for a multicultural society'
- Editorial: 'Getting it straight—what is anti-racist multicultural education?'
- Ray Chatwin asking: 'can ESL teaching be racist?'
- Alan Mathews on 'The dilemma of opposing values'—where there is conflict between them and their external community
- Paul McGowan: 'a bilingual education programme for Birmingham'
- Brenda Addison: 'group work in the anti-racist classroom'
- David Ruddell: 'Setting up 'multi-cultural working parties' in schools
- Trisha Wick: 'SATisfactory? National assessment and bilingual pupils'

Given our developing context, I wonder whether our education system could benefit from such a journal now. It would be easy to produce, maybe through the collective effort of the schools, colleges and universities. There are many schools in Birmingham who have a great deal of experience in effectively educating Pakistani children. There are even more who are new to the task. For example, we have some schools who say "prayer request from Muslim students; no problem" and they may even provide proper *wuzu*, ablution, facilities while others think it a strange idea. Sadly, the latter schools then end up making this 'normal' matter into a problem for themselves and their community. A journal of this type could provide a useful platform for sharing practice between our schools.

The education practice in the 1980s was guided by the Multicultural policy. This was a comprehensive 35-page, policy. It outlined three very clear aims:

> *To be aware of and to counter racism and the discriminatory practices to which it gives rise*

> *To be aware of and to provide for the particular needs of pupils having regard for their 'racial', ethnic, cultural, historical, linguistic and religious backgrounds*

> *To prepare all* (original emboldening) *pupils for life in our multicultural society and build upon the strengths of cultural diversity.*

The policy document did not leave anything to chance. It provided a rationale and gave details of the journey so far. It went out of its way to emphasise that the policy was equally necessary for all-White schools as it was for those which had a multi-racial population. It explained the concepts of racism and White privilege and pointed out that:

> "*There is racial inequality in Britain because in the main white people exclusively control most positions of management, government, influence and power; black people are disproportionately represented in menial work or have no work at all.*"

> "*. . . there is racial injustice in Birmingham because the practices, procedures and customs which determine the allocation of resources do discriminate, directly or indirectly, in favour of the white majority and against minority groups.*"

Quite helpfully, it then went onto spell out what the desired opposite would look like, using, according to the practice at the time, the term 'black' to mean all ethnic minorities:

> "*There will be racial equality when black people participate fully in all levels of society and the economy, and are therefore proportionately involved in management and government.*"

And, given its particular target audience, it pointed out:

> "*It follows there will be racial equality in education when black people are proportionately involved in teaching and administration at all levels, in higher and further education and in streams, sets, classes and schools leading to higher and further education.*"

The policy outlined that all children had the need to: "know who I am, where I come from, where I fit in and how and the need to succeed." It also explained what was meant by the different aspects of children's background. It provided a number of action checklists. In my view, the above is more than ever relevant for our education and the wider system. I would simply wish to replace the word 'black' with 'Pakistani'.

A time for leadership; the Birmingham Stephen Lawrence Commission

> *"What happens when people of different ethnic origins, speaking different languages and professing different religions, settle in the same geographical locality and live under the same political sovereignty? Unless a common purpose binds them together, tribal hostilities will drive them apart. Ethnic and racial conflict, it seems evident, will now replace the conflict of ideologies as the explosive issue of our times."*—Arthur Schlesinger[21]

Thanks to the tenacity of the Lawrence family, the last century ended well for race relations. After the murder of their son, Stephen, they campaigned tirelessly for justice. As a result of support from across the nation, including right wing newspapers, pressure had been applied on the government to do something. So, when Labour came to power, it decided to investigate not only the death but also to identify the lessons which could be learnt for the future. It decided to set up an inquiry under the chairmanship of Lord Macpherson. Later, resulting from the inquiry report, we were to have the Race Relations Amendment Act 2000, which was to put on the statute books some of its recommendations.

When the national report was published, the City Council decided to investigate the local situation by setting up the Birmingham Stephen Lawrence Commission (hereinafter Lawrence Commission). Chaired by District Judge Ray Singh, it was asked to:

> *"To examine the implications of the Stephen Lawrence Inquiry conclusions for Birmingham and to make recommendations on how the organisations responsible for combating racial harassment/violence including the City Council, should respond to the recommendations contained in the Inquiry Report."*

The Commission held a number of meetings and invited contributions from across the city. Some of these were submitted in person while others in writing. We made a submission from The Forward Partnership, which suggested to the Commission that it should consider broader issues for the city such as: "who lives here and on what terms; what sort of city do we wish to create for our future generations and what values do we wish to promote as a city."

Using the above quote from Schlesinger, I suggested that, instead of difference, we should talk about what unites us. "What do we have in common with each other? Who is my neighbour in this city of ours? Is it people of my race, ethnic group, faith or those who live near me, whose children go to the same school as our children, who are my work colleagues, whose concerns are similar to mine and who fight the same causes as me"? There was also a suggestion that we must not neglect the needs of the White community when addressing race equality.

When the Commission report 'Challenges for the Future' was published, right near the start, one could not miss the heading: "*Things are not working.*" This seemed to sum up what the commission had been told by the many staff of the City Council and the wider Birmingham community. It pointed out some unpleasant truths:

> *Under-representation in the political structures is mirrored in senior management positions in the institutions.*

> *There is no police officer of minority ethnic origin above inspector grade in the West Midlands Police Service*

> *Of the 8 Cabinet Chief Officers in the City Council, there is no one of minority ethnic origin.*

> *Two of the 13 Executive and Non-Executive Directors on the Board of the Health Authority are of minority ethnic origin*

> *Of the 10 Chief Executives in the health Trusts in Birmingham, currently, there is just one from a minority ethnic background*

Under-representation in City Council employment

The commission pointed out that as well as a general problem of under-representation, ethnic minorities were concentrated in lower job grades. In terms of the Council's minority ethnic workforce, it was pointed out that there were "some service departments with significant under-representation" with "only 4 out of the 13 Council departments" having representative profiles. Submissions from the Council's Black Workers groups and minority ethnic employees had drawn attention to "old boy and social networks" which "allow individuals whose faces fit to flourish and for those that do not to remain stagnant." It was pointed out that "individuals who have access to these networks are primed for career development opportunities." Later, when talking about institutional racism within the Council, it was pointed out that "senior White managers were uncomfortable about minority ethnic staff's experiences and showed little understanding of empathy with the way these staff feel."

A number of the submissions suggested that minority ethnic staff were often too fearful to complain about racism; afraid that they might be victimised and possibly lose their jobs. With my experience in employment, including with the City Council, and expertise in equality and diversity, I can understand what this means and how the process can work. Ethnic minorities can suffer twice—once with a problem and then with a lack of appropriate response from their seniors and the institution generally.

Having set and achieved a global target in 1989 to employ 20% ethnic minority staff across its workforce, at the time of the Commission, the Council had set differential targets in order to address under-representation by particular ethnic groups:

CHALLENGES FOR THE FUTURE

Table 14 Annual Improvement Target

Ethnic Group	1991 Census	Workforce 31.03.00	Difference	Annual Improvement Target (2001/2002)
Bangladeshi	1.3%	0.3%	-1%	1.3%
Black African	0.3%			
Black Caribbean	4.7%	8.5%	+3.5%	8.5%
Chinese	0.3%	0.1%	-0.2%	0.3%
Indian	5.3%	3.4%	-1.9%	5.3%
Other	2.7%	4.5%	+1.8%	4.5%
Pakistani	6.9%	2%	-4.9%	6.9%

Source: Birmingham City Council Central Personnel Services

The Commission report was launched at Austin Court in the centre of the city, on 22 March 2001. Present at the gathering were the then Leader of Birmingham City Council, Councillor Sir Albert Bore, Chief

Executive Michael Lyons and Judge Ray Singh who had chaired the Commission. Councillor Bore said:

> "The City Council commissioned this report because it wanted independent critical scrutiny of how key institutions in the City—including the Council—are tackling racism"

> "The Report has taken up from the Macpherson Inquiry the issue of institutional racism. And while I would accept that there are examples of institutional racism in some areas of the Council that quite emphatically does not mean that the Council is institutionally racist as an organisation." [22]

Much work still to be done

A year later, the same panel was brought back to review progress. In his foreword, Judge Ray Singh said:

> "We believe that the City Council must be seen to be leading from the front. If other organisations do not see the Council mainstreaming and prioritising race equality issues, this could have a knock-on effect in other sectors"

Although, the panel had not realised, all the boxes had already been ticked—report had been launched, discussed at key meetings, action plans produced—and everyone had moved on to their next priority. Their findings, contained in the report, 'The Challenge is Now' would best be summed up by paraphrasing their own original assessment—'Things are still not working':

> "Amongst representatives of the Black workers Groups within the City Council there is an ongoing perception of institutional racism and racial discrimination"

> ". . . Gender and disability issues are being addressed as a priority over race equality because these were considered to be more comfortable issues"

"There was a belief that at a management level race equality issues were not a priority and not actively pursued . . ."

"The City Council is and will continue to be the body to which other partners will look for an example"

To remove any doubt about inaction, the reconvened panel stated:

". . . There has been little progress since the publication of Challenges for the Futures. This view is held within the community, amongst staff who have been consulted, amongst some senior managers and by some Council members. It is a view that cannot be allowed to become a reality. Things must change."

At the launch of the original report, Councillor Bore had presented it as an example of the Council's commitment to race equality:

"We have a real and genuine commitment to combat discrimination and harassment and the Council has given public evidence of its commitment by . . . commissioning this Report."

That was over 10 years ago. What is the situation now, especially for the Pakistani community, which is my concern here? Have our institutions "woken up" to the Pakistani presence in the city? Birmingham, which has the largest Pakistani population in the country, could lead the way in showing how this presence "can be a key driver in building a successful and creative city."

It was acknowledged by the Commission that people needed to be treated equally as well as differently. This is very true for the Pakistani community. They need equality with other communities and respected for their differences.

PAKISTANI-BIRMINGHAM; THE CURRENT PICTURE

"Birmingham is currently home to the largest number of Pakistanis in the world outside Pakistan and is set to become the first majority Muslim city in Europe"—Department of Work and Pensions[23]

Research from the Barrow Cadbury Trust has indicated that by 2026, Pakistani presence in the city is likely to be 21%. "This increase is likely to be driven by the existing demographics of Birmingham's youthful Pakistani population rather than migration."[24] If we were to add to this those who do not show up in official statistics, then the figure could be 25%. As well as numbers, the economic disparities were pointed out between communities. The research stated that whereas a White male earned £332 per week, his Pakistani counterpart earned only £182.

According to the Department of Work and Pensions (hereinafter DWP 360), the size of the Pakistani community in Birmingham is 153,000. With the decrease amongst White and Black Caribbean, it is clear the city is becoming more Asian, especially Pakistani and more Muslim.

Pakistani employment in Birmingham

The following data shows the number of employed from the top five ethnic groups, for all employers in the city[25], making clear the Pakistani under-representation:

White British	269980
British Indian	21964
British Pakistani	20342

Black Caribbean   18674
White Irish   11416

Pakistani employment by Birmingham City Council (as at June 2012)

Black or Black Caribbean   2551   13.50%
Asian or Asian British   1705   9.02%
Pakistani   727   3.85%

The above figures are out of a total workforce of 18900. Out of the 727 Pakistanis, 534 were employed on Grade 1-3, 197 on Grade 4-5, 25 Grade 6-7 and 2 on the JNC scale.

The City Council has made excellent progress in employment of ethnic minorities in general and, in particular for Black Caribbean and Indians (who, I believe make-up most of the Asian or Asian British group). But much more needs to be done to improve the situation with reference to the Pakistani community. In 2001, the then Acting Head of Equalities Bruce Gill had said[26]:

> *"In a city with the population as diverse as Birmingham, it is crucial that the employee profile of the City Council has to be in line with the profiles of our citizens."*

For now we can see that, whatever 'positive action' steps the Council has taken have not worked as far as the Pakistani community is concerned. The target of 6.9% for Pakistani employees was clearly not achieved in 2001-2002 as their current presence in the council workforce is only 3.85%. Since this statement and since the publication of the Lawrence Commission report, the under-representation of Pakistanis in relation to their presence the city's population has actually increased from 4.9% to 7.04%. 7.04%. The gap is even bigger (i.e. 9.65) if one were to compare these employment figures against the data from the most recent census which shows the Pakistanis at 13.5% of the city's population.

Birmingham—Council Business Plan and Budget 2013+

In November 2010, the Council published a draft plan, for consultation. I was a Council employee at the time. We were invited by the Chief Executive of the Council, Stephen Hughes to send in our *"views, comments and ideas to help shape, inform and refine (the) draft proposals to help the Council deliver a package of services that enables it to meet the financial challenges we face whilst protecting key outcomes for Birmingham."* I made a full response, working on it over the Christmas holidays.

In the final plan, it is stated that "Birmingham is, outside of London, the UK's most diverse city, made up of a wide range of cultural, faith and other communities." We are informed that "the city benefits from positive social cohesion . . . . through working with all our communities, as well as with our public and private sector partners to address inequalities in our city"[27].

The Business Plan reiterates that "promoting equality and tackling inequalities is at the heart of the current Council goals" as is "building . . . a fair society." It then moves from mere words to actions. It explains the extreme importance of what was being done and left no doubt that if the task was to be achieved then it would require everyone's efforts. This was MAINSTREAM work, about this there was no doubt.

It is made clear that:

> *"The Council believes that addressing inequalities and disadvantage in the city is the responsibility of us all, and doing so is essential if we are to maintain social cohesion between and across all our communities. Equality underpins the City Council's guiding principles of freedom, fairness and responsibility. But in the end, it will take all of us working together to continue to build the strong, modern and fair Birmingham that we all want to see."*

Later, it is pointed out that it is the "responsibility of managers to ensure that equalities considerations are taken into account ***as part of*** (original emphasis) decision-making by elected members and Chief Officers."

So what is the problem? Reading the above declarations makes it difficult to see what Abbas or the Pakistani Network complain about Pakistani exclusion. The current ethnic make-up of the Council workforce is given above. I do know that in the area of education I worked until 2011, there are hardly any Black and Asian or Pakistani staff left. And this is a team of people who advise schools on such matters as underachievement and equalities.

Within the current staffing structure, there are nearly 60 top level posts. The six or seven at the very top attract salaries around £153,000. Below this level, the posts, at deputy chief officer level, attract salaries upto £117,000.

My purpose in including the salary information here is in the hope that there are Pakistani young people in our schools, colleges and universities who may be thinking of a career in local government. It certainly seems a world away from what they could make, even in a good week, as a taxi driver or waiting at tables down the Balti Triangle! I hope next time a teacher asks her class of Pakistani pupils what they want to do when they leave school, at least a few might say: 'I want to be the Chief Executive of Birmingham City Council' at a salary of £220,000.

Multi-ethnic leadership for a multi-ethnic city!

How long before this top level of the Council, with the most senior jobs and probably the highest salaries in the land reflect the ethnic make-up of our city? At least 4 would need to be held by Pakistanis, with a few more on top to be filled by other Asians, Black and other minorities. Are there staff on the lower rungs of the Council who would one day move up into these levels? As for Pakistanis, we have 25 on Grade 6-7. Will some of them move up into the higher echelons of the Council? A colleague who knows the city well pointed out that we are increasingly becoming male-dominated, and not just in the Council. She said it's as if the equality laws were never enacted. The question this raised for me, in the tradition of the Women's Movement: how long before we will see a Pakistani sister in the top post at Victoria Square or indeed in any one of the many senior jobs in our city.

On March 19, 2004, an editorial in the Birmingham Post had pointed out that "cultural diversity needs more than talk"[28]. The accompanying article by Jessica Shepherd had suggested that Birmingham should set an example for other cities. It was time, according to the newspaper for in-depth research in order to find out why "in a city where the ethnic minority population stands at 30 per cent, (it has gone up since then; to 47%), representation in well-paid managerial jobs is so disproportionate."

Paul Dale, in his front page article, had pointed out that "not a single management job . . . has gone to applicants of Pakistani or Kashmiri origin." The Evening Mail on the same day pointed out: "Employers must make every effort to ensure that their workforces—including senior posts—reflect the population. It's a huge challenge, but if we want to maintain our proud reputation for harmony we need to start finding solutions to a serious problem which won't go away." Suffice it to say that there is no need to write similar articles now, other than to point out that the situation has become worse.

Council's intentions on Equal Opportunities

> *"Birmingham City Council is committed to ensuring equality of opportunity in employment for everybody. We take action to avoid discrimination and take positive steps to redress the imbalance in the workforce profile. Job applicants are considered only on their ability to do the job for which they are applying"*[29]

According to its current policy (24 August 2012), the City Council is "committed to ensuring equality of opportunity in employment for everybody." That is, everybody, whatever race or ethnic background people are, including the Pakistani community. This kind of statement has been with us since the 1970s when we had the Sex Discrimination Act 1975 and Race Relations Act 1976 put in place.

The statement goes onto say that they "take action to avoid discrimination" and that they "take positive steps to redress the imbalance in the workforce profile." It would be worth taking a look at the details of what actually happens. Later it is stated: "The Council will undertake, through positive action, as set out in legislation, to address the issues of under representation." This is still one of the most misunderstood concepts related to equality and discrimination. Whenever one mentions it, most people hear positive *discrimination*. They think it means giving preferential treatment to ethnic minorities, especially over and above better qualified White people. Even some employers, who should know better, have such misunderstandings. My main question is directed at the City Council as a leader for Birmingham: **what is currently being done to address under-representation and to redress the imbalance that there may be between ethnic groups, especially Pakistanis?**

The Council says that "applicants are considered only on their ability to do the job for which they are applying." So, who they are, who they know, which social network they belong to, that sort of thing does not come into it. It is purely on the basis of their ability to do the job!

So, it is all above board. There is no 'giving jobs to one's friends' because one feels more comfortable working with them. There is a belief at work which says that some people may not fit in with other workers. Research by Richard Jenkins pointed out that it was not enough for applicants to be just suitable for jobs; they had to be *acceptable* too[30]. Do such arguments of suitability and acceptability still apply, I wonder?

EDUCATION FAILURE

"Educational underachievement is preventing the Pakistani heritage young people to realise their full potential . . . . This problem in Birmingham needs to be investigated and barriers must be removed. The Pakistani heritage community must have better input and more participation in the management of educational institutions" Pakistani Network

"Pakistani heritage pupils represent (one of) the largest ethnic groups in the City so any improvements in (their) attainment . . . will have a significant impact on Birmingham's overall performance"—City Council[31]

Our system seems to be fixated on percentages. Consequently, Pakistani young people are neglected. If instead we were to focus on actual numbers, we would realise that each year a very large number of them—around 1000—leave Birmingham schools without the benchmark qualifications or no qualifications whatsoever. Do we know what happens to these young people? What kind of future do they face upon leaving compulsory education?

I have been gathering such data for more than 10 years. During this time, some 10,000 Pakistani boys have left Birmingham schools and gone onto we-don't-know-what. We should find out. Based on our knowledge of the consequences of educational failure, it is very likely that many of these young people will have gone onto a life of crime.

There is talk of a drug problem in Birmingham's Pakistani community. I wonder how many of these boys, now men, are at the heart of the problem. Prison data shows us that around 13% of its population are Muslims and around 7% of Pakistani heritage. How many of them are our city's ex-pupils? We should embark on a research project to talk to the Pakistanis in prison or with a prison record and look at their life and especially educational trajectory. How did we as a city fail them? What could we have done to give them a different trajectory? More critically, what can we learn from their experience which we can use for the benefit of current and future generations? Taking no action is not an option. We would not want to look back in 2020 with an even larger number of failed students.

As late as 2001 Birmingham City Council was saying that the Pakistani underachievement would sort itself out in due course so there was no need to do anything about the problem. The Lawrence Commission report had pointed out that "Pakistani pupils will soon show rapid improvement as generational factors work through" (p 17). What was the basis of their claim when all the signs were pointing to a catastrophe, slowly developing in front of us? Their own evidence on the following page had shown Pakistani boys to be second from the bottom of a table for GCSE performance.

The following year, we had Birmingham Race Action Partnership (BRAP), the body whose role was to promote equality for *all* groups, tell Parliament that the only problem of educational underachievement affected Black Caribbean and Bangladeshis. There was no mention of Pakistanis. Joy Warmington, BRAP's Chief Officer pointed out to the House of Commons Education and Skills Committee, on 17 September 2002:

> "What we are looking at over the next ten years is a significant growth in the Bangladeshi population but they are one of the lowest achieving groups in Birmingham, especially Bangladeshi boys."

She explained that BRAP was "the equivalent of a race equality development agency for Birmingham": "We focus primarily on race and racism and how it manifests itself within some of the key institutions of Birmingham. We work with the institutions to try to put together practical interventions that can help to bring about mainstream change." She pointed out that they did not just work in education and took "a joined up strategy around race equality" She pointed out that their partnership was funded and supported by a number of organisations with the purpose of challenging them. "We are not owned by any one partner. We do not get embroiled in the politics of having to bow to the master or the person funding us."

The Council has taken little or no specific and targeted action to improve the situation of Pakistani underachievement.

I hope to be in a better position to comment on this after the completion of my current research into Pakistani boys' education in Birmingham.

Ethnic minority pupil, teachers and governors in Birmingham Schools

Pakistani pupils in Birmingham schools have increased from 16.7% in 1995 to 24.5% in 2011[32]. This is a huge increase. After English, Urdu and other Pakistani languages (Mirpuri/Pahari and Pashto) have been identified as 'home language' by the largest number of young people in Birmingham schools i.e. 22027.

It is not beyond the realm of possibility that there will come a time when Pakistani pupils will become the largest ethnic group in Birmingham! What happens to them has massive consequences for the city.

ETHNIC COMMUNITIES OF BIRMINGHAM PUPILS 2011

	Primary	Secondary	Special	All
	%	%	%	%
White British	36.0	40.1	46.2	37.9
White Irish	0.6	0.9	0.8	0.7
White Other	2.4	2.2	1.6	2.3
Mixed	6.8	6.6	7.4	6.7
Indian	4.9	6.4	2.9	5.5
Pakistani	26.0	22.6	21.3	24.5
Bangladeshi	5.6	5.1	3.5	5.4
Asian Other	1.4	1.3	2.0	1.3
Black Caribbean	4.9	5.1	5.6	5.0
Black African (Somali)	3.1	2.5	2.3	2.8
Black African (Excl Somali)	2.5	1.9	1.8	2.3
Black Other	1.2	1.0	1.1	1.1
Chinese	0.4	0.4	0.3	0.4
Any Other Ethnic Group	3.3	2.8	2.1	3.1
No Information	1.0	1.0	1.1	1.0
Total	100	100	100	100

Based on compulsory school age pupils excludes PRU data

Teachers employed by Birmingham Education

"Improving the representation of minority ethnic teachers is fundamentally important. Minority ethnic teachers provide important role models for minority ethnic pupils." Lawrence Commission

The City Council has acknowledged that there is a current imbalance between the demographics in the teaching workforce and pupil population.

> *"Locally evidence indicates that some 156,408 pupils . . . of which 78541 (50.2%) are from Black and minority ethnic groups. However, this is not reflected in the teaching workforce as only 11.6% of teachers are from BME background"*[33].

There continues to be under-representation of Pakistanis amongst the school workforce. For example, according to the City Council data, in 2003, less than one per cent of those employed in leadership roles were Pakistani. They were 1.6% of the teaching workforce, 4.3% of classroom assistants and 1% of learning mentors. The teacher presence had gone up slightly from 2001 when the Lawrence Commission had shown it as 1.13%.

As at 31 August 2011, there were 1774 Pakistani employees within schools. It is not clear at what grade they are employed or the number who are teachers as opposed to being in support or admin roles.

There is a clear need to recruit more Pakistani staff in our schools in order to create a 'reflective' workforce i.e. with reference to 43427 Pakistani pupils in Birmingham.

Pakistani governors in Birmingham educational establishments

> *"At a minimum, there should be a clear expectation that each governing body is representative of the ethnic composition in the school* (and college and university)." Lawrence Commission

Each of the schools, colleges and universities has a governing body. Governors are drawn from parents, staff and the wider community. Using data from a range of sources I have tried to paint a picture of the situation in the city (Annex 3).

For local authority schools, currently, there are 170 Pakistani governors out of a total of 5111. To reflect the current Pakistani pupil numbers, we would need over one thousand more governors from the community.

According to Greg Cox there is "deficient" monitoring and recruiting and retaining strategies. He also sheds important light on the processes involved. "People not fluent in English experience an atmosphere that tends to favour professionals who have a full grasp of the jargon associated with the education process. Many people from ethnic minorities feel that they are not taken seriously because they have limited English and are simply unable to put their point across effectively. As a result, many only attend a few meetings and then drift away"[34].

Greg Cox recommended that "bilingual training and support should be available to minority ethnic governors." I wonder whether, in schools which serve a mainly Pakistani community, could governing body meetings be held in the community's own language or other creative solutions found so parents are not excluded on grounds of their inability to speak fluent English. He also recommended that research should be undertaken to establish the link between pupil progress, employment of minority ethnic teachers and parental participation in school life. It would appear little has been done in response to these recommendations.

King Edward Foundation schools and Academies

A small number of Birmingham schools are listed on the *www.whatdotheyknow.com* site. This includes the grammar schools within the King Edwards Foundation. For the three I was able to obtain data, they have between 12-15% Pakistani pupils, around 1% Pakistani staff and no Pakistani involvement on their governing bodies.

Also, listed on the above website are the newly established academies. These new schools are independent of the City Council and each one has a business sponsor. I was able to obtain data for only a few such academies. North Birmingham has 15% Pakistani pupils and 2% Pakistani staff while Heartlands has 34% Pakistani pupils and 13% Pakistani staff. As for people on their governing bodies, I have been informed by their sponsor, E-Act, that they do "not centrally record the ethnic or racial backgrounds of its governors."

Pakistani presence in colleges of further education

Through Freedom of Information, I have gathered data on a number of colleges. For example, Birmingham Metropolitan College has 15% Pakistani students, 2% Pakistani staff and just one Pakistani on their governing body who happens to be a student. According to their Ofsted report (2 February 2011):

"They promote equality and diversity strongly and achieve high levels of educational and social inclusion"

"They have not resolved persistent underachievement by certain groups of learners from minority ethnic backgrounds."

"Success rates by learners aged 16 to 18 from Pakistani, Mixed White and Asian and Any Other backgrounds and by adults from any Asian, Black African and Any Other background are low and have been so for some time."

For Joseph Chamberlain Sixth Form College, the majority of its students are from the Pakistani community; 12% staff but only two out of eighteen governors are from the same background.

Solihull Sixth Form College has 14% Pakistani students. They have 3 Pakistani staff, out of 298 and 1 Pakistani on their governing body, out of 19. According to their Ofsted report (7 October 2011):

"The largest group of minority ethnic students is of Pakistani heritage"

"Although, students of Pakistani heritage, as at the time of the previous inspection, achieve lower success rates than other students."

"Equality and diversity are satisfactory. The college has closed the gap in success rates between most groups of students, but that between students of Pakistani heritage and other students has increased"

Cadbury Sixth Form College has 20% Pakistani students, 17% Pakistani staff and one Pakistani governor. According to their Ofsted report (16-19 October 2012)

"The student population mirrors the ethnic diversity in the city with approximately a third of students of White heritage, a third of Asian heritage and one fifth of Black heritage"

"Inequality between the achievements of different groups of students is declining as gaps in achievement between most are closing . . . .

The achievement gap for students of Asian/Pakistani heritage is not closing sufficiently quickly"

After nearly forty years work in equalities, I am completely baffled how, according to Ofsted, a college can have persistent underachievement by its largest ethnic minority group, the Pakistanis, and yet still be "doing well" in terms of equality and diversity.

For the Adult Education Service, the situation is best summed up by these extracts from their 2012 Equalities report:

"Black and Minority Ethnic groups are well represented in our learner population, with learners of Pakistani origin being the largest minority group."

"The two profiles (staff and students) *differ most significantly in respect of the 'Asian—Pakistani' group, which comprises 17% of learners, but only 4% of staff."*[35]

On 11 April 2013, I was informed that "it is not Birmingham City Council's policy to recruit any particular ethnic groups unless it is a business need for any particular role." How does this square up with the City Council's employment equality commitment, mentioned above where it was stated: "take positive steps to redress the imbalance in the workforce profile."

I hope this book will reinforce, the already obvious, business case so that Pakistani staff can be recruited, in proportion to the students from their community.

Pakistani presence in higher education (especially Birmingham University)

For my generation, getting to a university, any university, was an achievement. Although it still is an achievement, the trouble is that now there are many more people with university degrees. So it's not enough anymore that you have a degree; it has to be in the right subject, from the right university. This is a point that is often lost on parents who have not been to university themselves. There are many of them in the Pakistani community.

According to the data I have been able to gather, the largest number of Pakistani students are to be found at Aston University, at 8%, followed by 7% at Birmingham City University. They both employ around 2% Pakistani staff. However, as a case study, I have decided to focus on Birmingham University

Young people from across the country and even the world fight to get a place here. It is known as a 'Redbrick' university. There are 6 such universities. The others are in Liverpool, Leeds, Bristol, Sheffield and Manchester. Generally, it is considered that a qualification is worth more if it is from one of these universities. Its annual income in 2007-08 was around £400,000,000.

With student numbers around 25000, Birmingham University is the largest in the West Midlands. It is ranked as one of the top 10 universities by employers of people with degrees. So a degree from here is certainly worth having.

In its response to my Freedom of Information request, the university has stated that in 2011-2012, 759 (2.74%) of its students identified themselves as of Pakistani ethnicity. 459 of these were in Social Sciences and Medical and Dental Sciences combined. I don't know how many of these students are British Pakistani. It is possible that some of them are citizens of Pakistan and who will return to their country upon completion of their study.

Birmingham University Governing body

The university has a Council which is, made up "of 24 members drawn from the University's management, academic and student communities and the lay community." 16 of the Council are described as 'lay members' who are "individuals who bring external experience and perspective to Council. They are neither staff nor students of the University. They are usually appointed following advertisement and interview, and serve to four years in the first instance."

In response to my request for information on how many Pakistanis they had on the Council, I was told that "the University confirms that it does not hold data collectively on the ethnicity of Council members and therefore cannot provide information in the context of the request."

Looking at the University website[36], I could see that one of the lay members of its Council is of Asian origin; Dr Ranjit Sondhi BSc, OBE.

Mr Sondhi was a community activist when I first met him in the late 1970s; he had founded and led the radical Asian Resource Centre in Lozells. On the university's website, we are told that he is "currently Chairman of the Heart of Birmingham teaching Primary Care Trust and a Civil Service Commissioner." Also, that he has been appointed as "Board member of the Tenants Services Authority, Member of the National Leadership Council of the NHS and as an Ambassador for Diversity on Public Boards." The list goes on:

> *"He is currently also Chairman of Sampad, a South Asian Arts organization, and a Trustee of the Baring Foundation and Bryant Trust. Recently appointed as a Visiting Professor for Cohesion, Diversity and Intercultural Relations at the University of Coventry."*

For a number of years, Mr Sondhi was a Governor of the BBC. It is good to see that people like him are now a part of the Birmingham establishment. We just need a few more to bring the representation in line with the presence of all our ethnic groups, especially the Pakistanis.

Birmingham University—a place of work too

As well as being a place of study, like schools and colleges, universities are places of employment. The jobs are not just academic and teaching:

> *"The University of Birmingham is one of the largest and most diverse employers in the region, with around 6000 staff working in a range of academic, professional, technical, manual and clerical roles."*

> *"Our staff have come from across the region, the country and the world to work with us, not only because of our outstanding academic reputation, but because of the culture of innovation and forward thinking that is part of the way of life at Birmingham."*

Being a large modern employer, this comes across a very attractive and worthwhile place of work. An array of benefits is on offer to its employees. These include: pensions tailored to meet the needs of staff;

generous holiday entitlement for support, administrative and other related staff; work-life balance and private medical and dental schemes.

The university states its commitment equality. It states that "staff are drawn from over 16 ethnic groups and 95 countries." Its staffing data is very comprehensive indeed, with over 99.2% disclosing their personal details. The current data shows:

> "15.4% staff are from Black, Asian or other minority ethnic groups and 83.8% staff are from White ethnic groups"

> "Asian staff (Indian, Pakistani, Bangladeshi and other Asian ethnic groups) make up the largest proportion of the Black and minority ethnic staff, at 6.9% of the total staff population, with Asian-Indian staff the single largest at 4.4%"

> "The largest proportion of Black and minority ethnic staff are employed in Support roles (17.7)."

The university currently has 6257 staff. Out of this 75 are Pakistani, (1.2%), 25 of whom are employed in the College of Medical and Dental Sciences. 30 of the Pakistani staff are employed in Corporate Services. For a large and attractive employer in Birmingham which is proud of its diversity, there is clearly some work to do in relation to the employment of Pakistani community.

I have been informed, through a follow-up communication on 28 March 2013, that the "University does not currently have plans to increase the number of Pakistani heritage staff. However, it is planning to identify those groups who are under—represented on its staff and will then consider how it may target these groups."

'Birmingham'; more than a geographical location!

We hear about concepts such as Corporate Social Responsibility. How does this apply to these education providers? What responsibility comes with being a city-based organisation, especially as many very keenly use the name Birmingham to tell the world of their location? We know partnership between formal organisations and their communities can bring benefits for both. Are the colleges and universities missing a trick here, I wonder!

For colleges and universities, it seems the words 'further' and 'higher' also denote the distance that exists between them and the Pakistani community (disadvantaged communities generally?). My impression, formed over many years of living and working in Birmingham, is that there is also a continuum of 'distance' between educational establishments and the Pakistani community. With some exceptions, the more prestigious an organisation, the further it appears to be from the community. In Birmingham University's Alumni News (Spring 2013), the writer Dr Benjamin Zephaniah, poet and musician, talks about how he used to see the University as a "foreign fortress." I suspect that for many in the Pakistani community that is still the case.

We know a great deal of money is spent on research, including on inequalities. However, little attention appears to have been paid to the 'colour of the academy' itself i.e. the employment of Black and Asians, especially Pakistanis in academic and in senior roles. How long will it be before we see Black, Asian or Pakistanis as heads of universities?

According to a front page of Eastern Eye, 8 February 2013:

'Universities are racist'.

The article, based on a report from the University and College Union pointed out that there is only one minority ethnic person who holds the position of vice-chancellor at a UK university[37]. Could it be that our higher education sector is practising indirect racial discrimination? In any case, I wonder how much of the report applies to our local higher education establishments.

At the annual research gathering in 2012, held at Birmingham University, I asked a question about the lack of diversity in top layers of academia. The panel, three White and one Black, had little to say in response. However, one of the panel members, Dr Stephen Gorard, afterwards drew my attention to students who were 'missing' from higher education. I wondered what the figure was for his own, Birmingham University which had very few Pakistani-British students. This also reminded me of the 5990 'missing' Pakistani students nationally from the gifted and talented[38] and made me wonder whether and how the two groups were linked.

Can the subaltern speak![39]

I would be the first to acknowledge the contribution of White people who fought for equality and justice. This helped to create the conditions in which Pakistanis and other minorities could live their lives and sometimes flourish in places such as Birmingham. But, I believe the time has come not so much for passing the baton but for White people to share the space with minorities. The Pakistani community certainly needs to be an active participant when marketing and presenting our city to the rest of the world. Maybe then, the picture would be more multidimensional.

There was a time when Karl Marx's opinion, "they cannot represent themselves; they must be represented", may have been necessary but surely not now, after over 60 years of post-war migration. Gayatri Chakravorty Spivak posed her statement with reference to a subaltern, a British military term for junior officer, literally meaning a subordinate. The obvious question for me is: 'can the Pakistanis speak! Within the overall community, it is also necessary to pose a similar statement for women who are often denied a voice of their own.

Within our democratic society, the 'unrepresented' have the right to a voice. In any case, it is not wholly possible for outsiders to speak for a community; for an authentic expression people have to speak for themselves. We should no longer have, what the Lawrence Commission described as the 'observers of racism' speaking on key issues; it should instead be done "by those with firsthand knowledge and direct experience of racism and racial inequality." One particular place where this is necessary is within the academy. We should no longer have people with second or third hand knowledge to speak on subjects such as discrimination, bilingualism and racism. For minority people these are not just matters of theory learnt from second and third hand research; they are able to draw on personal experience. I wonder whether the time has come for the empire to strike again![40]

The absent presence of Pakistanis in research

Much of our knowledge locally is dependent upon national research where Pakistanis are but a small minority. With the exception of some negative issues, their absence is the norm and their presence an afterthought. If they do make an appearance, they are more likely to be buried within the umbrella labels of 'Black' and 'Asian'. I present two examples to explain the problem.

There was a national report produced on the engagement of fathers in preventive services. It interviewed 92 individuals in 13 centres: 40 fathers, 26 mothers and 26 members of staff. It was admitted that "most of the interviewees were white." The 8 parents and 2 workers from ethnic minority background covered "African, Caribbean, South Asian, Middle Eastern and mixed race." The researchers then admitted that the "diversity, taken together with the small total number involved, meant that it would not be methodologically sound for us to attempt to draw general conclusions about the experiences of interviews from minority ethnic groups."[41] Meanwhile, we have a large number of Pakistani fathers in Birmingham. Do we understand their situation enough? Has local research been conducted as a supplement to what is available nationally?

On another occasion a report was produced about decision-making of high achieving university applicants. On page 46 of the report, "the need for research on the impact of ethnicity" was acknowledged."[42] So, I wrote to the organisation suggesting they commission research on the matter. They replied: "We don't as a rule commission research specifically on ethnic minorities I'm afraid.

I could give numerous other examples. Wherever one looks (with the exception of terrorism and extremism!), one is led to the conclusion that labels such as 'men' 'women' 'parent' 'elderly' etc usually mean White. Of course, it's never said but that is exactly what is meant. It would be stating the obvious to say that there is a need for locally-focussed research on the Pakistani community on a range of subject matters.

In my PhD, I am conscious of being able to use my extra, bilingual, ear, and cultural understanding to conduct some of the research, with Pakistani pupils and their parents. It is possible that the paucity of Pakistani 'insiders' is one explanation why the community remains under-researched.

PAKISTANI HEALTH

Health inequalities also continue to adversely affect the community. There is higher incidence of diabetes, high blood pressure, heart disease and disability compared with other residents. Pakistani Network

Diabetes

One headline pointed out that ethnic minorities were twice as likely to suffer from diabetes as White people. This did not surprise me at all. My impression is that 'Pakistani' and 'diabetes' go together as naturally as fish and chips. The 'sugar' illness appears to be so prevalent in our community that people don't even talk about it unless they suffer from it more severally than normal.

On 10 SEP 2012, Lawrence McGinty, Science and Medical Editor for ITV asked: 'What's the biggest problem facing the NHS? Reorganisation? Cost Savings?' He then proceeded to tell people visiting his website about the disease, diabetes, which was costing the NHS almost £12,000,000,000 a year. He pointed out that it was about 10 per cent of the total budget of NHS and that it was going to get worse[43].

Professor Chaturvedi at Imperial College has researched this area. It was this that had led to the above and many other similar headlines. This showed Pakistanis as the worse affected group.

Then there are other health problems which the Pakistani community seems to suffer from. Smoking and its related illness, heart problems, being over-weight, mental illness, the list goes on. Are there particular strategies in place on these matters with the necessary resources and culturally competent staff?

According to Health Survey for England—Health of Minority Ethnic Groups 2004—, for smoking Pakistanis were 29% and Indians at 20%, for prevalence for diabetes Pakistanis were 17.9% while Indians were 9.8%. It also showed the trends for men in the period 1999-2004 and pointed out: "increase in diabetes—differs by subgroup (15% to 21% in Indians and 28% to 44% in Pakistanis, 5% to 7% in the general population)."

The House of Commons Health Committee report 2008-2009 has a very enlightening bar chart, on page 18, of people from different ethnic groups who suffered from poor health[44]. Looking at the chart reminded me of all the races we have been watching recently in the Olympics and the Paralympics. The chart showed Pakistani women reaching the finishing line, in this race to certain death, before any other group, just beating Bangladeshi women who came second. The Pakistani men were in 4th place, with Bangladeshi men in the third.

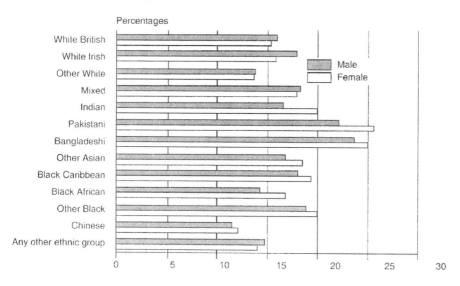

Age-standardised limiting long-term illness: by ethnic group and sex, April 2001, England and Wales
Source - ONS[13]

According to the report 'UNEQUAL LIVES, which maps health Inequalities in Birmingham's Asian communities', life expectancy varies between wards of the city[45]. Not surprisingly, top 5 wards were: Sutton Trinity (where people are expected to live till about 85), Perry Barr, Sutton New Hall, Sutton Four Oaks and Sutton Vesey (where they live till 80). These wards also had the fewest Asians living there compared to the rest of the city. And the bottom 5 wards were Sparkbrook (where they live till about 72) followed by Washwood Heath, Lozells and East Handsworth, Bordesely Green and Springfield (where they live till about 77 years). Not surprising to find that four of the bottom five wards are majority Pakistani areas.

The document also points out the following key facts:

- Asian communities have lower life expectancies (especially Pakistani and Bangladeshi men)
- Pakistani and Bangladeshi communities report the poorest health. Coronary Heart Disease and incidence of Type II Diabetes are much higher than national norms.
- Pakistani men and women are more likely to report acute sickness than the general population
- Pakistani men and women and Bangladeshi men are more likely than the average to score sufficiently highly on tests of psychological wellbeing to be considered indicative of psychiatric morbidity, although mental health and ethnicity is a complex topic.

It would be more accurate to say that we do not so much have a health problem with Asians in Birmingham but with Pakistanis (and Bangladeshis).

Urgent action needed

UNEQUAL LIVES says nothing as to what follow-up action is to be taken. In the chapter on 'Access to Health Services in Birmingham', under 'Identifying Barriers' it lists a number of barriers. These are identical to the ones found on the internet; authored by Dr Gurvinder Rull:

> *"The diversity of race, language, religion, culture and biological factors within and between people of different ethnic groups can produce inequalities and associated uptake of health services."*

> *"Communication and language are fundamental and clinicians have to be certain of understanding patients and being understood"*[46]

What is being done to make sure this understanding is there? Only then can appropriate action can be taken. It is stated that "culture and attitudes can affect many aspects of healthcare." This raises the importance of providing a culturally competent health service. A diverse workforce can help in this respect. This point is also made by the writers of the report: "Equally, it is important to understand cultural differences and attitudes so that effective healthcare can be delivered in a sensitive way."

Sadly, the report is quiet on what it proposes to do about the above barriers. At the least, we should try to understand them and find ways to overcome them. Otherwise, people (Pakistanis) will go on dying early or leading unsatisfactory lives. The report is also surprisingly quiet on discrimination, racism and Islamophobia. It is generally accepted that these 'social evils'[47] can cause health problems as well as act as barriers to accessing services. For example, those Muslims adopting 'visual identifiers' (beard, headscarf, even kameez shalwar) can face additional stress.[48].

In his foreword, Dr Ranjit Sondhi CBE, Chair of the Heart of Birmingham Teaching Primary Care Trust, has accepted what needs to be done:

> "What is needed is a recalibration of how we tackle inequalities in health. We must acknowledge how inequality is constructed and persists."

At the least, we will need to see plans to recruit more Pakistani staff, bilingual staff to overcome the language barriers, increased involvement by the community on the Boards of health trusts and hospitals, training for staff to make them more culturally and religiously competent and health awareness programmes for the local Pakistani (and Bangladeshi) communities. Specific research on racism and Islamophobia would also be worthwhile.

Pakistani involvement in the health sector

Strategic Health Authority

Quite surprisingly, I have been told that the Authority's staff are not required to declare their heritage or ethnicity as part of ethnic monitoring.

However of those that did declare their ethnicity, as of 27 September 2012, the Authority employs:

> 5 staff of Pakistani heritage—one at Band 2, two at Band 3 and two at GP Educator. This is 1.17% of the total workforce.

Birmingham Children's Hospital

Pakistani service users: 14%
Pakistani staff: 2.5%
Pakistanis on governing body   1 (out of 13)

Birmingham and Solihull Mental Health NHS Foundation Trust

Pakistani service users   7.56%
Pakistani staff   2.7%
Pakistanis on governing body   1 (of 22)

NHS Birmingham East & North

I made a Freedom of Information request and received a reply on behalf of the four PCTs: Heart of Birmingham Training PCT; NHS Birmingham East & North (including Birmingham Primary Care Shared Services Agency); South Birmingham PCT; Heart of Birmingham Training PCT. Between them, the Trusts have 106,000 Pakistani residents, out of 153000 Pakistanis in Birmingham.

When asked whether they had any Positive Action schemes in place to address under-representation amongst staff and details of any services which are targeted at the Pakistani community, I was informed: "All services are culturally competent and able to work with service users from the Pakistani community."

University Hospitals Birmingham

Pakistani Patients.   2.35%
Pakistani staff   2%
Pakistanis on governing body.   0

Workforce 2012

I was pointed to a website which contained the above report. Strangely, out of all the diversity categories, this section on ethnicity was the only one which did not have a comment or explanation from the writer of the report.

Quite helpfully, the Trust provides a chart which compares the ethnic origin of its staff with the ethnic makeup of Birmingham residents. There are a number of communities who are employed to a greater extent than their presence in the city. The reverse is the case for Pakistanis. They are the most significant group who are under-represented as employees compared to their presence in the city[49].

The chart below compares the ethnic origins of our staff with that of Birmingham City Council residents[3].

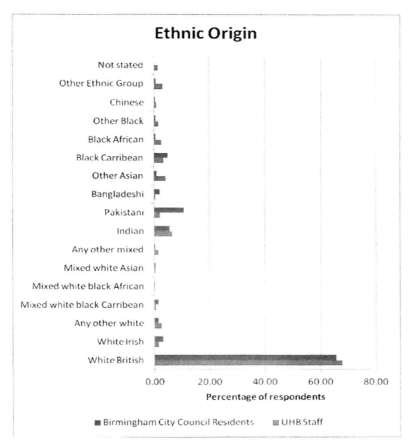

OTHER PUBLIC AND PUBLICY FUNDED BODIES

Pakistani employment in West Midlands Police Authority

The Police Authority sets annual local employment targets for the recruitment, retention and progression of police officers and police staff. For example, these set out how many officers progressing from constable to sergeant and how many should be from Black and minority backgrounds or women. Currently, the authority employs 1.57% Pakistani staff. Of the 208 employees, 118 are Police Officers, 42 other Police staff, 21 Police Community Support Officers and 27 Special Constables.

Pakistani involvement in key voluntary sector organisations

> *"Lack of voluntary and community infrastructure means that the community is not well placed to resolve its own issues . . ."*
> Pakistani Network

I include here three key organisations: Birmingham Voluntary Service Council; Regional Action West Midlands and Birmingham Race Action Partnership. I have referred to their websites in order to understand what they do.

Birmingham Voluntary Service Council

BVSC "is one of Birmingham's leading independent resources. It is the key voluntary sector support organisation in Birmingham and one of the largest such bodies in the UK." As well as providing a number of services such as volunteering opportunities and information and guidance, it works to "champion the voluntary sector as an influential force for positive change." It acts in a co-ordinating role for Birmingham's charitable sector, "ensuring that grassroots organisations, which have a unique insight into the realities of everyday living in the city, are represented at and scrutinise decision-making forums."

They have a contract with Birmingham City Council worth £544,728 over three years.

I have had links with BVSC over many years. I have also written articles[50] for their in-house journal Update. When I was seeking support for this report, BVSC were one of the organisations I had approached.

Ethnic minority staff	7 (out of 35)
Pakistani staff	1 (out of 35)
Ethnic minority Board members	5 (out of 14)
Pakistani Board members	0

We know from one of the BVSC reports, that 84% of third sector organisations have a policy on equal opportunities and anti discrimination[51]. Based on my many years experience as an equality practitioner, such policies are often not worth the paper they are written on. They can be downloaded from one of the many internet sites. As the Lawrence Commission reminded us, it is not the policies but their implementation and impact that matters. The policies have to be accompanied by a properly resourced action plan which is implemented and regularly reviewed.

When asked whether third sector employers kept data on ethnicity of their employees and service users, Brian Carr, Chief Executive of BVSC responded "that many do, but can't vouch for all in such a large and diverse sector . . ."[52] Richard Beard, Chief Executive of the Jericho Foundation confirmed the situation and said that "some organisations will keep ethnicity data of employees and service users but some wont unless it is a specific requirement of their funders"[53]

By far the largest provider of funds for these third sector organisations is the City Council. They clearly have a role to play in influencing equality developments within the sector.

Regional Action West Midlands

RAWM "exists to enable a sustainable, influential, effective and inclusive voluntary and community sector in the West Midlands area." Its current strategic aims include promoting and maximising "the contribution of the voluntary and community sector in improving the quality of life for disadvantaged communities" and to "be recognised as the support agency for voluntary and community organisations" and to "respond to the present & future needs of voluntary and community organisations in the West Midlands."

Pakistani staff	0
Pakistani board members	0

Birmingham Race Action Partnership

BRAP was established in 1998 as an independent organization. Its five founder bodies were all represented on its board: Birmingham City Council, Birmingham Primary Care Trust, Birmingham and Solihull TEC, Birmingham Voluntary Services Council and Birmingham Trade Union Council. This has been expanded to include University and private sector representatives. In its time, it was described as an innovative organization.

Currently, the organisation describes itself as a "think fair tank, inspiring and leading change to make public, private and voluntary sector organisations fit for the needs of a more diverse society." It would appear it is a service provider which "offers tailored, progressive and common sense approaches to equalities training, consultancy and community engagement issues." Its vision: "Making equality work for everyone" and its mission: "To help people, communities, and the organisations that serve them turn equality into reality."

BRAP also continues to be seen by others as having a strategic role in the city on diversity. Not long ago, I was at the AGM of a Birmingham organisation. Sitting next to me was the CEO of an influential Birmingham based umbrella organisation. S/he asked what I was doing in my work. I explained that my focus was diversity. I made reference to my then recently completed report, for the Department for Children, Schools and Families, on equality in service provision. I was hoping that we would go onto have a conversation about the report, its content, implications for places like Birmingham. But, no. s/he said words to the effect of "We don't do diversity; all that sort of thing is done by BRAP." I did want to say that diversity was everyone's responsibility but the meeting began and we started to talk about the Birmingham riots.

Pakistani staff	2 (out of 12)
Pakistani Board members	3 ("that's about 25%")

I then enquired about BRAP's membership and whether that included Pakistanis. Asif Afridi, Deputy Chief Executive Officer explained: "Our members are organisations—not individuals—so the question about Pakistani members isn't really relevant to us. We run a wide range of projects, many of which support Pakistani people, but none of our work is aimed 'specifically' at Pakistani people."

I then asked: "As you work with organisations, not individuals, am I right to assume that these 3 (Board Members) are representatives of, and mandated by, Birmingham Pakistani organisations? What sort of process do you go through for nominations and appointments?

He said: "No—they aren't representatives of and mandated by Birmingham Pakistani organisations. Board members appointed by application/ interview process"

The only question I would like to pose is whether the above three voluntary sector organisations represent Birmingham's Pakistani community? If so, how effective are they in doing this job?

PROCUREMENT OF SERVICES
BY BIRMINGHAM CITY COUNCIL

Councils such as Birmingham have a number of duties to provide services. Some of these they are not able to provide themselves but have to procure or buy in from other providers. For this, the Council keeps a standing list of approved contractors and suppliers. They will have been assessed as being suitable for such work. The Birmingham list has over 500 names on it.

Alongside value for money, the Council is concerned that businesses who deliver contracts for it abide by all the same equality requirements that the Council itself has to deliver. This is a legal requirement and has been for some time.

To make sure the contractors deliver on equalities, the Council, with the West Midlands Forum, has developed a Common Standard for Equalities in Public Procurement (hereinafter the Equalities Standard), (Annex 4) for assessing whether Council contracts meet the requirements of the Race Relations Act 2000 and observe the Commission for Racial Equality's Code of Practice in Employment. The West Midlands Forum consists of 6 Councils, including Birmingham City Council.

The Standard lays down what employers who wish to win contracts for work should do in terms of equalities. In 2002, a report was written by Warwick University[54] to evaluate the standard. The report has been a major source of information for this section.

With particular reference to Birmingham City Council, I have been informed that:

"*All suppliers are required to meet the West Midlands Forum 'Common Standard for Equalities in Public Procurement'. This covers all aspects of equalities including gender identity and sexual orientation.*

This is set at different levels—5, 5-49 and above 50 employees—as it recognises a proportionate response as this is just one part of documentation during a tender process.

This standard is in respect of their employees. Where a contract is citizen facing then there is liked to be reference to and requests for method statements on their approach to equality and diversity issues as part of the quality evaluation. The 'value' this has in the evaluation with vary to the nature of the tender. E.g. the proposed home and residential care contracts have the following two clauses:

> *The Provider shall have a strong commitment to equality of opportunity at all levels throughout the service to avoid discrimination and shall, where relevant, take **positive steps to redress the imbalance in the workforce profile** (my emphasis).*

> *The Provider shall ensure that Employees are made aware of its policies in relation to treatment Service Users including Equal Opportunities, safeguarding, Mental Capacity Act and use of dignity and respect, and are appropriately trained and monitored in line with the provision's relevant Service Specification.*

Extract from Standard Tender Documentation referring to equalities.

13.10 <u>West Midlands Common Standard for Equalities</u>

13.10.1 The Service Provider shall within three months from the Contract Commencement meet the standards required by the West Midlands Common Standard for Equalities in Public Procurement.

1310.2 For the duration of the contract term, the Service Provider shall maintain the standards required by the West Midlands Common Standard for Equalities in Public Procurement.

13.10.3 At any time during the Contract Term, the Service Provider may be subject to monitoring in respect of the West Midlands Common Standard for Equalities in Public Procurement. The Service Provider will co-operate with the Council in meeting the Council's monitoring requirements. Where Council monitoring indicates that any part of the Service Providers Equality Policy does not comply with the West Midlands Common Standard for Equalities in Public Procurement, the Service Provider will make such alterations as are reasonably required to its Equalities Policy in order to comply with the Council's requirements.[55]

Contractor equality in practice

By using *www.whatdotheyknow.com* I requested from the City Council information on a few of the larger and key contracts delivered by private and third sector companies. This included: the value of contracts; the contractors' equality policy; number and percentage of their employees who are of ethnic minority background, especially from Pakistani heritage; Positive Action strategies which the companies have in place to address recruitment of under-represented ethnic groups and percentage of ethnic minority/ Pakistani heritage board members the contractors have.

AMEY

The Birmingham Highways Maintenance & Management Contract is worth around £2,700,000,000 over 25years.

Ethnic minority employees

Total head count from Birmingham by location addresses is 1166:

Asian	12.6%
Black	0.26 %
White	67.6%
Pakistani	2.5%

Positive Action strategies

In response to a question about their Positive Action strategies, I was told: "The Company recruits based on merit."

This is a very interesting response. The concept 'Positive Action' has been with us since 1975. It is stating the obvious to say that it does not have any intention to go against the merit principle. It did not do then, nor does it do so now. When it was first introduced, it encouraged and permitted such activities as pre-recruitment training and advertising in ethnic minority press.

The law has now taken the concept a little further though still very much within the merit principle. Under the current legislation, Equality Act 2010, if there are two candidates for a job equally qualified then the employer can give it to the person who is from an under-represented group. So, Amey need not have any worries about abandoning the merit principle. No one is asking them to appoint, in this case, Pakistanis, if they were not up to the job. To do so would be against the law.

I would further advise that the Company take a serious look at what they can do within the legal framework which might help them to increase the employment of Pakistanis from the quite abysmal numbers they currently employ.

Pakistani board members

"There are no Ethnic Minority executive team members on the Birmingham contract."

Inclusion Policy

This was supplied. It states: "Our aim is to remove any barriers for employees . . . ." What barriers are there and how will they be removed? Is there a strategy in place to investigate and take remedial action? It is pointed out that the Company strives "to attract talent from the widest possible pool available." It then goes onto remind us that they are committed "to the principles of a meritocracy." This would indicate that the Company believes that somehow attracting talent from the widest pool available is in some way against the principles of meritocracy.

It states that the Company will not tolerate unfair discrimination. How does it know when discrimination takes place? Is there monitoring of its processes and systems? Is there a system to allow staff to flag up problems? Do managers understand what discrimination looks like and what to do when it occurs? There is talk of suppliers. What is their commitment to equality for Pakistanis? Are there any Pakistani owned businesses who are suppliers in this context?

It is stated that "all managers involved in the recruitment and selection processes will undergo appropriate training in Equal Opportunity and Diversity awareness." The Company may wish to improve its understanding of Positive Action. It will then realise that taking such action does not mean compromising the merit principle.

The Company talks of maintaining "records in recruitment, training and employment and use this information as a means of identifying and remedying any areas of inequality." What action has been undertaken to identify under-representation of Pakistanis?

There is some indication of the Company's desire for its workforce to be "in line with the working population mix in the relevant labour market areas." So does this mean that one day we can expect Amey to employ Pakistanis in proportion to their presence in Birmingham!

ATKINS

I was told that the 7 year contract with Atkins formally ended on 30th April 2012. The City Council now use a government framework where Atkins is one of several suppliers of consultancy services. I was told that the "information on ethnic makeup of the workforce is not something we would collect or collate as we are limited in our dealings with suppliers to asking certain prescribed questions which are directed toward establishing that the Company is compliant with legislation."

LEND LEASE

This Company won the Birmingham schools building contract; valued at £176,896,168.

Equality Policy

It is the briefest of the policies. Under discrimination and the promotion of equality, it says they will not "discriminate directly or indirectly . . ." That's it! No mention of promotion of equality. So, they will not break the law.

Together with Catalyst and Birmingham City Council, the Company forms the Birmingham LEP (local education partnership). They published a plan and invited comments from the public. Here are a few extracts from my response:

The failed 31484

The above figure gives us the number of Birmingham students who, between 2007-2011, did not achieve 5 A*-C at GCSE with English and Maths. The two largest ethnic groups were White (14678) and Pakistani (6502).

Good news is that the numbers of the failed are going down, slowly. There were 7384 of them in 2007 and had gone down to 5110 by 2011. The bad news is that those who are failed by the school system go on failing throughout their lives, unless of course, something is down about it. This is where the critical role of second-chance further and adult education provision can make a real difference; something for the LEP to consider.

Independent equality assurance

The LEP was 'quality assured' by Birmingham Professional Divercity in 2009 as announced in the press notice on their website. In my experience, it is very easy to satisfy criteria that are set by in-house experts whose actions can be affected by local 'influence' from their funders. Given the size and nature of the LEP, it would be advisable for the organisations involved to be assessed externally in order to assure independence, objectivity and greater robustness.

As a minimum, given that the LEP is a contractor for a public body i.e. Birmingham City Council, it ought to be expected to satisfy the requirements of the Equalities Standard. It would also be advisable to refer to the government advice on Public Sector Duty which, because of its contract with a public body, now applies to the LEP. At the least, the LEP would wish to meet the minimum expectations. Given that Pakistanis will soon become the largest ethnic group in the schools being built, the LEP may wish to show leadership in a city-wide Positive Action programme aimed at the Pakistani community.

CARILLION

There are two contracts with this; one worth £145,000,000 and another worth £4,436,222.

Equality Policy

We are told that the Company has a full equality and diversity policy and that they will make every effort to "ensure that all employees are treated with courtesy, dignity and respect irrespective of gender, race, religion, nationality, colour, sexual orientation, disability, age or marital status."

We are further told that Carillion have a strategic objective to "attract, develop and retain excellent people by becoming an employer of choice." They wish for their Company to "reflect the diverse society we live in. One example of enacting the policy is our focus on training and employing people who are jobless, homeless or ex-offenders."

In response to my questions about the number of Pakistanis they employ and whether they have any Positive Action strategies in place to deal with any under—representation in their staff, I was told that "Birmingham City Council have not included any requirements in Company our contract for monitoring or employing specific minorities or backgrounds—as such we do not collate any such data for reporting on these contracts." So, where does this Company stand in relation to the Equalities Standard?

MARKETING BIRMINGHAM

The value of their contract is £2,500,000 per year. The current contract runs until 31 March 2015 to enable (Marketing Birmingham) "to act as the strategic marketing agency."

The Company employs 8 ethnic minority staff, of whom 2 are of Pakistani origin. This is 3.2% of the workforce. I was informed that there are two Board members who are of "ethnic minority background."[56] The organisation does not have a Positive Action strategy.

According to its equality statement, the objective of the organisation is "that our work, services and employment practices will promote a positive impression of the city and we will take every step to minimize or eliminate outdated preconceptions and stereotypes." It leads one to wonder what is done in relation to Pakistani-Birmingham (other than with reference to balti restaurants!) and how is it achieved with so little Pakistani input in the form of staff and Board membership! In my view concepts such as 'Cultural Imperialism' and Orientalism[57] are very relevant here as is Spivak posing the question: who speaks for whom?

And yet the Company claims that it "whole-heartedly supports the principle of equal opportunities in employment and opposes all forms of unlawful or unfair discrimination on the grounds of colour, race, nationality, ethnic or national origin, sex, disability, age, religious belief, sexual orientation or marital status." Furthermore, it is pointed out that the Company is "committed, wherever practicable, to achieving and maintaining a workforce which broadly reflects the local community in which we operate." I wonder whether they have considered the implications of this commitment in the context of the large Pakistani presence in Birmingham.

MIDLAND ARTS CENTRE

The 2012/13 contract value is £650,000. I was informed that the City Council does not hold information on whether the organisation employs any Pakistani staff or has any Pakistani Board members.

EVERSHEDS LLP

The total spend by the City Council with this Company, between 8 January 2010 and 9 October 2012, was £363,297.64.

In their equality and diversity policy, there is an advertisement. Under the heading 'It's not what you are, it's who you are', it is pointed out: "We have become one of the world's largest law firms by hiring world class people, whatever their backgrounds, perspectives or beliefs." They talk of a workplace "where everyone gets the chance to reach their full potential."

At the end of their policy, they provide data on their employees, as at January 2009. This points to there being 4% Asian and 0.4% Muslim (also shown as 0.3%). This was a surprise to me given that law is a popular profession in the Pakistani community.

SEVERN TRENT WATER LTD

Their current contract is worth £5,376,000. I was told the City Council "does not hold any data on the staff of Severn Trent Water ltd or their policies."

AGE CONCERN

Their current contract is worth £224,144 for prevention of depression following bereavement. Does this include work with the Pakistani community? Again, I was informed that the "Council does not hold data on the staff of Age Concern or its policies."

Other suppliers to the City Council

On its website, the City Council provides details of payments to suppliers. For November 2012, the payments are included in Annex 5. The key questions are whether these suppliers comply with the requirements of the Equalities Standard and the number of Pakistanis they employ.

THE PRIVATE SECTOR; AN EVEN MORE SERIOUS CAUSE FOR CONCERN!

"Are we becoming, or have we become, a starkly segregated city with a predominantly White prosperous business sector, with minority communities largely excluded from all but manual and clerical positions, a First World and Third World Birmingham?"
Citizens Alliance

In 2004, the report: 'Cause for concern—Is Birmingham's Private Sector Failing Britain's Second City?' was produced by the organisation Citizens Alliance—"a broad-based coalition of diverse faith and community organisations in Birmingham working in relationship on issues of common interest." It set out to survey the ethnic diversity within the private sector, by contacting 58 Birmingham employers. The majority were "in the sphere of professional services, law, finance, consultancy and property and feature some of the most prominent company names in the city." The significance of the sector was shown up by this quote: "the professional sector expects to expand by up to 50,000 jobs in Birmingham and Solihull by 2010."

Only 8 companies responded to the survey. But four of them did not want their information to be made public. Negative responses such as 'we are too busy' or 'not able to help' were received from 10 companies and no response at all from 40. The report pointed out that "at present the White population occupies at least 80% of the jobs in the professional services sector . . ."

It referred to the 'Post People' pages of photographs which appeared in the Birmingham Post each week of the business sector and its celebrations, charity events, launches, anniversaries and promotions. "The people whose images appear in these photographs are almost entirely White." It posed the rather direct and obvious question: "what does this tell us about racial justice and the social and economic health of the city?"

Elsewhere, the report pointed out that "even in companies that are taking the issue of ethnic diversity seriously and are making progress, people from ethnic minorities are concentrated overwhelmingly at the bottom of the private sector labour market." We were told that it was not all bad news as the report listed HSBC, Severn Trent plc, West Bromwich Building Society and Birmingham Post and Mail Ltd as companies "who are leading the way on ethnic diversity in the private sector."

The Citizens Alliance had asked employers to take Positive Action to address the problem. It gave a few examples of the kind of steps which could be taken."

What is the current situation in the above four companies? Has the list become longer over time of those with effective practice? Have any companies taken Positive Action as suggested, if so, to what end? What is the situation of Pakistani employment in the private sector in the city generally?

A Sunday paper profiled students who were getting ready to go to university. It was with the view to see the impact of the £9000 fees being charged by universities. I don't know how this has impacted on the Pakistani young people and their families. Knowing the community with their commitment to the education of their children, they will do whatever they can to send them to university.

Reading the paper, one story caught my eye. It began; "A frisson of fear may trouble many a student as they embark on life at university under the £9,000 fees regime this autumn. Not so for Davika (not her real name), as she starts her accountancy course at Birmingham University. The reason is that it will all be paid for by her employer, KPMG." Given the firm has a Birmingham presence, I wondered how many Pakistani students were similarly having their fees paid so they could attend this course at the university which has a central place in our city's life.

The limited information I have been able to gather about private sector companies would point to an even more serious cause for concern compared to the situation outlined in 2004. If this is the state of affairs in companies which are under some pressure from the public sector to address equalities, address equalities, I seriously worry what it must be like in the rest of the sector.

For the City Council, does more need to be done to make sure that it complies with its Equality Duty? Otherwise, there could be a danger of large contracts being awarded to companies where its policy on procurement is not being applied and the Equalities Standard being disregarded.

It may be helpful to remind ourselves what the Lawrence Commission said on this matter: "(there is a) requirement for procurement policies to be tied to equality consideration and to be supported by arrangements to ensure compliance . . ."

In 1898, the Fabians (Tract No 84) were making a case for moral behaviour by businesses who delivered contracts for local Councils. This was a time when much of what a Council needed was delivered by contractors and value for money was often the only consideration. It was argued at the time that it was no business of the Council what an employer did, who he employed, for how much and under what terms and conditions.

Things have changed now. At least, we have laws in place telling us what we should do. The Essential Guide to the Public Sector duty from the Equality and Human Rights Commission advises that contractors' performance on any equality conditions in the contract should be reviewed through regular meetings. It says that the purchasing authority (the Council) should make clear, in the tender documentation, what information it needs for the contractor to collect and report on. Then, it should act promptly if there is non-compliance "as you may be liable under the general equality duty." Also, in such situations of non-compliance "public authorities may want to seek to identify the reasons for it and work with the contractor to rectify the problem"

According to the Department of Work and Pensions, in Birmingham only 24.8% of Company policies included a specific focus on race and even less so, 21.6%, on religion. So, that's over three quarters of our city's employers who do not pay any attention to race or religion in their equality policies. Meanwhile, Muslims (alongside other faith communities) have pointed out that the government and employers are not doing enough to respond to their needs[58].

In 2005 Tahir Abbas, University of Birmingham and Muhammad Anwar, University of Warwick[59] pointed out that there was "little evidence that big employers or service providers in Birmingham see race equality as a mainstream activity." Two of the largest recent contracts the city has awarded involved the rebuilding of our schools and the New Street

Station. I wonder how much of the money was used in employing city's Pakistanis or using this community's businesses. Will the situation be any different in the future?

"Leading campaigner talks divercity"

The following are extracts from the above press release from Birmingham Future which outline this organisation's view on diversity.

> *". . . it is clear that the business community currently does not reflect the demographic make-up of the city"*

Chris Robertson, chair of Birmingham Future and partner at Deloitte, said:

> *"One of Birmingham's strongest assets is the diversity of its population."*

> *"The professional and financial services sector has remained predominantly White—a situation that does not represent the ethnic make-up of our city. At the same time, many ethnic minority led businesses are thriving in the city and yet are not fully recognised in this sector. As a result Birmingham businesses are missing out on a great pool of bright and talented individuals."*

> *"By just respecting and reflecting the culture of your customers via your staff, you can help your business flourish and open it up to a range of diverse and broader market groups."*

Richard Johnson, executive director of Birmingham Professional DiverCity, said:"

> *"The demographics of our city are changing as the majority of the city's younger generation belongs to an ethnic minority group."*

> *"Birmingham Future is ideally placed to tackle the issue and will appeal to the younger generations too."*[60]

The above event took place on 10 August 2005 and was hosted by Ernst & Young. It had marked the first diversity event of Mr Robertson's year in charge, during which he had pledged to put diversity at the top of Birmingham Future's agenda.

Is the future likely to be fairer?

There has been discussion of what would make Birmingham fairer[61]. I believe it would be a start to treat fairly the second largest ethnic group in terms of employment, service provision and governance. But this will require more than a surface response based on a colour and difference-blind and universal approach to equality as at present. Instead, it will need to be a targeted and differentiated approach which takes account of different needs, circumstances and histories of our communities.

Firms wishing to conduct business with Birmingham City Council are being asked to sign a social responsibility charter[62], with a clear hint that those refusing to do so may not win contracts with the local authority in future. Will it mean greater fairness for the Pakistani community once firms have signed up to the charter which includes the following all encompassing, 'one-size-fits-all' statement?

> *"Not discriminate in respect of recruitment, compensation, access to training, promotion, termination of employment or retirement based upon race, caste, national origin, religion, age, disability (including learning disability), mental health issues, gender, marital status, sexual orientation, union membership or political affiliation."*

THE CRIMINALS AND THE INNOCENT

A few years ago, Lord Nazir Ahmed was remembering the good old days when it was seen as shameful if a Pakistani family had been visited by the police for anything negative. He said such an event was seen to bring shame on the whole community. Words would be had with the culprit, by the family, by the neighbours and at the mosque. "But times have changed."[63]

'*Persons and vehicles searched*' data, for 2011-12, courtesy of West Midlands Police Pakistani Reference Group, showed 36763 'stop and searches', of which 16929 affected White British. In second place were the Pakistanis, at 5994 (3559 for 'drugs', 1027 'going equipped' 780 'stolen property' 581 'offensive weapons' and 47 for 'firearms').

Without a doubt, the most worrying figure was the one for drugs which placed the Pakistanis only 2668 behind the large White British. It reminded me of a similar 'closeness' in the schools data (see chart). In both cases, it is conceivable that the Pakistanis will in the near future take the lead; unless, of course, we do something about it.

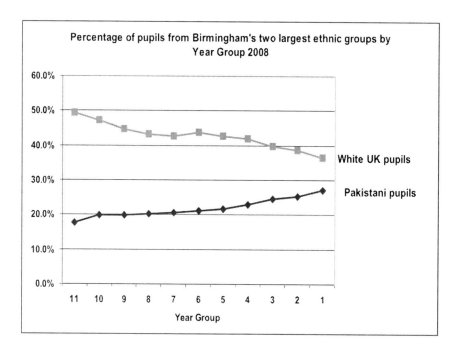

I have another set of figures, also courtesy of the same source. This showed the 'stop and search' data 2010-2011. The overall figure for West Midlands Police was 39906 out of which 6737 were Pakistanis. But the figures which caused me serious concern showed that in the Birmingham East area, out of a total of 8977 arrests, 4088 were Pakistani. It is likely that some of the arrests may have involved innocent people. If so, this must leave an even more of a nasty memory for those arrested and their families and friends.

Location of responsibility

The Pakistani community is familiar with the phrase 'Do More!' It is generally used in relation to the 'war on terror' and the West's expectations of Pakistan. I came across a version of it being used here in Birmingham. At a community gathering, according to the Urdu newspaper, The Nation (18 January 2013) a senior official of the City Council said words to the effect of: "we acknowledge the very positive contribution of the Muslims. However, the community and organisations such as the Muslim Council of Britain need to do more to address the problems of drug dealing and prostitution amongst the young in inner city areas." This reminded me of the following quote from Marta Bolognani:

There was trouble in a street and the police contacted the mosque. I don't know how it happened, there was representative of the mosque, police person and there were youth, so the police said to the mosque chairperson, 'you need to look after your lot' and what the response from the mosque chairperson was (I found it amazing): 'This is not our lot. This is your lot. It comes from your schooling system, from your system, from your society, it is not my lot, it is your lot. My lot is me, my age group. We came, we never went into crime, so don't tell me this is my lot, this is your lot. You have done this'. So it was very interesting, I just happened to hear. Do you understand? 'It is your lot, it is your lot, because this is the product of this system, I haven't agreed to this system' (Tahir, teacher in his early forties)[64]

Birmingham Community Safety Partnership

According to the Home Office, these partnerships are made up of representatives from the police and Police Authority, the local Council and the fire, health and probation services. They were set up as statutory bodies under Sections 5-7 of the Crime and Disorder Act 1998. All the agencies work together to develop and implement strategies to protect their local communities from crime and to help people feel safe. They work out local approaches to deal with issues including antisocial behaviour, drug or alcohol misuse and re-offending. They also work with others who have a key role, including community groups.

I thought, given Pakistanis are a large community in the city and are affected by crime, both as victims and perpetrators; I would investigate the extent to which the community's perspective is included in the organisation's work. So, I submitted a Freedom of Information request. Their response is given below:

- "The organisation does not employ any Pakistanis"
- "The organisation does not have any Pakistanis on its governing body."
- "The organisation does not record the ethnicity of their service users"

Is it too obvious to suggest that the Partnership links up with some of the religious leaders mentioned above as well as others, preferably on their terms and speaking their language?

PAKISTANIS IN THE BIRMINGHAM PICTURE

Throughout much of my life in the UK, I was of the view that how we saw things in the West was universal. This was how everyone saw it. Furthermore, our way of seeing the world was the right way. If others did see things differently, then they were wrong, for our way was rational and objective and they were not only irrational but biased and quite simply wrong.

But, then slowly my education improved. At the time the book Satanic Verses came out, I was very much a part of the secular world. When all the protests began to take place across the country and then in other counties, I began to think that maybe, just maybe, there was another way to understand things such as freedom, offence and religion.

The second time I was made to think about different world views was after that terrible day in 2001 when the Twin Towers were hit. At the time, as a Diversity Consultant, I worked for a large private sector company, advising them on a range of issues. I recall being told by them that some of their Muslim employees were refusing to respect the 'one minute silence'. Apparently, they were saying that no such silence had been held for many other occasions when people had lost their lives such as in Palestine or Kashmir.

On the 10th anniversary of 9/11, I read in my Urdu newspaper, a comment from a Birmingham Pakistani writer. He was wondering whether, in all the activities and the events that were to take place, there was going to be anyone also remembering the many thousands of lives which had been lost in places such as Afghanistan and Pakistan as a result of the 'war on terror'. I have my family home in Kashmir; I have a sister who lives in Peshawar, only a few miles from Afghanistan. There are many Brummies who have personal connections with other parts of Pakistan. I remember some of my City Council colleagues being really upset because their fellow staff had not shown any interest in the Kashmir earthquake.

I have also been encouraged to see the world differently by Edward Said's *Orientalism*. The West's perspective which is the central plank of his book may have been fine at the time but now requires a review. At the time the West and the East were supposedly worlds apart (never the twain etc) but things have changed somewhat with the movement of peoples we have had especially since World War II. Many of the people of the East, the 'Orientals', are no longer somewhere else but are actually a part of our world in the West. They (or should I say we as I belong to that world, having been born in the Orient and now being very much a part of the West's fabric) cannot be talked about as 'foreign', 'other', 'outsiders', 'pariahs'. We are here, as a poster from the Institute of Race Relations once pointed out, "because you were there."

The Black philosopher Charles W Mills65 has pointed out the obvious. He has said that people like Karl Marx, John Stuart Mill, John Maynard Keynes and Adam Smith were all White. At first I thought "of course they were. You would expect that given they came from a White country." However, it did make me wonder why we see such people not as 'White' but as 'normal'.

Mills went onto remind us that how these people saw the world was biased. They saw it from the White, Western viewpoint. Again, that is exactly what you would expect as they came from the White West. The trouble is not with where they were born or their race but the fact that we are constantly being told that they were Universalists, that their view was the world view. Perhaps it is time for the young in our schools to learn from other perspectives too. What is taught about the Bengal Famine when millions died who could have been saved? What about the Jallianwalah Bagh massacre? What is taught about the political mess that was Partition or that is still Kashmir? What about the very biased position that Lord Mountbatten took against Mr Jinnah and Pakistan? How could these have been handled differently? Here in Birmingham we certainly need something broader than the parochial teaching of history being imposed currently on our nation's youth by our government and their favoured advisers.

Ethnic terminology and histories

Elsewhere, I have referred to the use of the term 'Black' by race activists to describe all non-White communities, including Asians, as if they were one homogeneous group. There had been little consultation with or involvement of the people affected. Many Asians saw themselves according to their national origins and religion. For many, little changed while the activists and the sociologists and others made assumptions about them.

We would benefit from undertaking a review of the terms we use to describe our communities. It certainly does not make sense to use the term 'Black' to describe Asians. Furthermore, it would be sensible to unpick the term Asian when we discuss matters such as educational underachievement, health inequalities and employment exclusion because Asians differ in the extent to which they are affected.

As with any large community, there are bound to be other differences, of social class, region, linguistic etc. So, I would go even further and suggest that we start to unpick the term Pakistani given the size of the community and the diversity within the community ('we are not all the same', I was told by one Pakistani).

Black History Month has effectively placed Black heritage on our national agenda. I believe the time has come to build on its success. I am not suggesting that we abandon it; it's far too valuable for that. Rather, that we review it and come up with something that includes all our communities' histories. I would also like to propose that we mark dates such as 23 March (Pakistan Day) and 14-15 August (Independence days for both Pakistan and India).

The Pakistani Network and the Birmingham mentoring organisation, Pioneers, have produced an excellent leaflet on Pakistani history. Entitled 'Prominent Leaders of the Pakistan Movement 23 March 1940', it lists:

Muhammad Ali Jinnah	Allama Muhammad Iqbal	Maulana Muhammad Ali
Fatima Jinnah	Maulana Shaukat Ali	Sir Syed Ahmed Khan
Choudhry Rahmat Ali		

I would like to propose that Birmingham schools are issued with copies of the leaflet to encourage the study of the people listed. Other, similar resources could also be commissioned.

Only some recognised!

A few years ago I undertook a project to produce biographies of Birmingham Asians. My aim was to have men and women, young and old, from all the main Asian communities. The people chosen were a reflection of my limited knowledge of our community. It included the following:

Ranjit Sondhi	Tahir Abbas	Jagmohan Joshi
Tony Huq	Rama Joshi	Mohammed Ayub
Jaswinder Didially	Javed Khan	Deepak Naik
Anita Bhalla	Dr SA Khan	Abbas Shah
Naseem Akhter	Mahmood Hashmi	Wasim Khan

The biographies were posted on the website **www.emaonline.org.uk** which is a resource for schools. Sadly, none of them or indeed any other Asians have made it to the list of the 'Famous People from Birmingham': **www.birmingham.gov.uk/famous-people**. It includes the following 'great' and the 'good':

Edward Burne-Jones	George Cadbury	Joseph Chamberlain
Tony Hancock	Ozzy Osbourne	JRR Tolkien
John Henry Newman	Jane Loudon	David Cox
Albert Ketelbey	Alec Issigonis	Arthur Neville Chamberlain
Arthur Conan Doyle, Sir	Graham Paul Webb	H. V. Morton
John Baskerville	Michael Balcon, Sir	Major John Hall-Edwards
Matthew Boulton	Joseph Priestley	James Watt
Hilaire Belloc	William Withering	Mary Anne Schimmelpenninck
Jane Bunford	John Bright MP	Michael Balcon,
Sir Sid Field	John Baskerville	Washington Irving
John Cotton	Samuel Johnson	Jasper Carrott
Benjamin Zephaniah	Francis William Aston	Edward Augustus Freeman
Duran Duran	Roy Wood	Judith Cutler
Lindsey Davis	Steve Winwood	

As well as this list, another way that we mark our city's famous people is through the Blue Plaque scheme of the Birmingham Civic Society.

We also have the Lunar Society and the Chamberlain Forum. I have written to them to find out about Pakistani involvement in their activities.

In speaking to the staff of one of the three 'civic' bodies, I was told, "never mind the Pakistanis, the trouble with us is that we are a mainly Edgbaston and Harborne organisation."

I certainly know that when the Lunar Society was set up it was intended to be an inclusive organisation. According to Jenny Uglow, they were united by a common love of science, which they thought sufficient to bring together persons of all faiths and none. They said they would welcome Christians, Jews, Muslims and Heathens, Monarchists and Republicans. I wait to find out the Society's current membership to see whether it indeed continues to be inclusive of all the people of Birmingham as its founding fathers had intended.

I attended a presentation at the Council House by the local Historian Jahan Mohammed on Pakistani contribution to the world wars. It was very informative and a joy to see so many Pakistanis in the Council Chamber; one even made his contribution in Urdu. This made me think that we have made tremendous strides as a society to accommodate the needs of people with a disability who need signers. Could this be used as a model to provide interpreters for people whose best and preferred language of communication is something other than English?

Solomos and Back talk about Councillor Phillip Murphy making a proposal, in January 1990, that there should be translation of Council speeches in Urdu and Punjabi. The proposal was given a hostile reception. Murphy had said:

> "We are talking about making Birmingham an international city, and here we have a City Council with a large ethnic population and it seems to me it would show them a tremendous respect."

The really critical point, at the above history meeting, was made, by a member of the audience during the Questions and Answers session. He said: "Let us tell our children what our ancestors did for this country." I think he was talking about Pakistani children learning about their ancestors' contribution to the two wars. I wouldn't just focus on the wars but also all the Pakistani sweat that went into the rebuilding of Britain and Birmingham during the 1950s, 1960s onwards. Also, I would broaden such learning to all Birmingham children so they appreciate the contribution of communities such as Pakistanis beyond providing curry. While sitting in the Council Chamber, I wondered why none of the City Council staff were at the event.

In 1986, Danielle Jolly produced a report, one of the first of its kind, where she researched the views of Pakistani parents about their children's education. She found the parents making a case for teaching White children about Pakistani culture. They thought this would lead to better understanding:

> *"They should be taught (Pakistani culture), so there would be a better understanding, if they know our culture and our ways, there wouldn't be as much hatred as there is now."*

> *"They should be taught our culture also; then there would be better understanding and there would be a bit of love in their heart for us and they would think that we are good human beings and we are coming from a good country."*[66]

Chris Palmer wrote, in Multicultural Review about racist bias history teaching:

> *In a nutshell, then, History as it is traditionally taught is elitist, sexist, ethnocentric and racist. A history course can sail through 300 or so years of history via Drake, Raleigh, Cromwell, Marlborough, Wolfe, Nelson, Wellington and the like with only a passing reference to women and non-European peoples and countries.*[67]

Mr Palmer went onto explain bias through both omission and commission. Does this still hold true of history teaching in Birmingham schools?

We cannot look at that great wartime leader, Churchill, without reference to his own racial prejudices or continue to present Jinnah as the bad guy when we are surrounded by large numbers of Pakistanis who owe their existence to his courage and perseverance. I believe it is time for a reconsideration of what is taught in Birmingham schools. What perspectives and biases do the teachers have, having been brought up on our Orientalist education system?

When the world wars are covered in the curriculum, what do the children learn about the Indian contribution? Of course, there was no Pakistan or Bangladesh then (as I often have to explain to pupils and occasionally to teachers). During their work on the British Empire and, in particular, the British rule in India, what are they taught about all the good that was done? Are they also taught about some of the bad? Would the students be taught something about the horrors of Jalianwallah Bagh when General Dyer completely lost his mind and ordered the killing of hundreds of innocent civilians? How did the mainly Indian soldiers feel having to carry out the orders of this mad English man who was getting them to kill their own people?

Or what do the students learn about the million plus people who were allowed to starve to death during the Bengal famine while Britain watched and its leader blamed the victims for "breeding like rabbits."

PAKISTANIS IN THE BIRMINGHAM MAIL

I wanted to find out whether Pakistanis were in our city's picture. Where better to look than the Birmingham Mail, the main daily paper for the city with a circulation of some 50,000 per day.

I consulted the newspaper over a four-week period, 15 October-10 November 2012. My aim was to gain a general impression of the type of picture the newspaper paints of Birmingham's Pakistani community. I believe newspapers such as this have a very important role to play. They can educate people about their neighbours, good and bad, with their multidimensional lives. I considered: what is said, what is left out; who writes it—an outsider, or someone with an insider's perspective of the community; who is used as the expert; how much space is allocated to what topic and where in the paper is it placed.

My general impression was that there are no Pakistani journalists employed on the paper though one of the four Asian sounding names could have been Pakistani. Therefore, much of what was written about the community was by 'outsiders', that is, non-Pakistanis. This is not to say that only someone from within the Pakistani community can write about the community in Birmingham. However, with some exceptions, just as in academic research the job is done much better by an 'insider' so it is in the media; someone from within the community is more likely to bring a more authentic perspective. Such people often have a 'third eye' and an extra ear to see and hear things which others don't. According to the Society of Editors "if minority communities are to be properly understood and provided for, Black and Asian people, from different cultures and religions, should be represented on their staffs and among managers."[68]

Reading some of the 'human interest' articles made me wonder about all the similarly interesting people we have in the Birmingham Pakistani community. What are the chances of seeing the details of their lives in the pages of the Birmingham Mail!

During this period, the paper provided detailed coverage of Malala Yousafzai, the 15 year old Pakistani girl from Swat who had been shot by the Taliban. After the shooting, she ended up at the Queen Elizabeth Hospital in Birmingham. She became a cause célèbre for the world's media. Of course, like in all such situations, we are not able to unpick why this person became the focus on this occasion in this way. We know she is not the only girl or person who is shot by the Taliban. We also know there are many innocent civilians, young and old, who have lost their lives at the hands of the Western forces through, for example, the drone attacks. Very few of them are written about by the West's media.

There was coverage of a Remembrance Day Weekend event at Golden Hillock School which involved the opening of a memorial garden. I wondered whether there are any aspiring journalists at schools such as this who serve the Pakistani community and who could be encouraged by the newspaper.

There was a two page article under the headline: 'The best is yet to come'. This was an article, with pictures, of the US election won by Barack Obama. There is an election coming up in Pakistan in 2013. Many in the local Pakistani community will be involved and even more will be interested in what happens. We wait to see what kind of reporting and insight will be provided in the pages of the paper. The item 'Brum Head's OBE honour' was about Kamal Hanif being awarded by the Queen. From the heart of the Pakistani community, this is exactly the kind of stories we need to see more of in the local mainstream press.

There was an 8-page feature entitled 'Halloween Horrors' with pictures sent in by the public. On another occasion there was a two-page feature 'Birmingham at Christmas'. Could we have had similar coverage of the recent Eid festival which fell during the period in question but you wouldn't have known it from the paper. It would have been very easy to tell the readers where and at what times the Eid prayers were being said.

This particular Eid festival could be a rich source for stories of local people going on the Hajj pilgrimage. Sadly, some of the pilgrims are also taken advantage of by fraudsters. Again, that would provide stories. Then, there was a very warm, two-page story, about an English couple who had been married for 70 years. There must be many couples in Pakistani-Birmingham who have equally been married for a long time.

Buried in the corner of one page was 'Nun praises kind cabbie'. This was the story of a Catholic nun being stranded. Her plight was noticed by a cabbie who took her to her destination. "He wouldn't take the fare", said Sister Mary. "He said he was a Muslim and that was his good deed for the day. I don't know his name, but would like to thank him. It was very kind." There must surely be more such stories in and around Birmingham's Pakistani community. These could be used to provide a balance for the many negative stories that appear.

There was an item with Tony Robinson and Jack Dromey MP on a tour of ExtraCare complex in New Oscott. Dromey was quoted as saying that ". . . we have an obligation to those who built Birmingham and Britain to ensure that they have security and dignity in retirement." The same could be said of the thousands of Pakistani elders in our city. Where would our city be without their backbreaking work in our factories and foundries? However, I am not sure how many Pakistanis end up at the ExtraCare complex.

On one occasion there was an article 'Why were 60 trains cancelled or delayed?' Otherwise an ordinary report but very special because there were two pictures of annoyed customers. One of whom was Diane Evans and the other Yasmin Akhtar, with her headscarf. For me it summed up what I believe we need more of; news of Pakistanis and Muslims in the city as ordinary, multi-dimensional human beings.

There were very few examples of Pakistanis making an appearance in the paper as 'expert'. Khalid Mahmood MP was an exception. He was pointing out that children were being put at risk in Birmingham.

Grosvenor talked of "a consensus between the local political elite and the local press that Black people in Birmingham constituted a 'problem'." He spoke of White politicians and officers in Birmingham having preferential access to the media "and thereby exercised control over public discourse." Meanwhile, the Black population in Birmingham had to "surmount significant barriers to have their views heard."

During the four-week period of reading the Mail, I learnt little about Pakistani-Birmingham for the community barely made it into the frame. It was noticeable by its absence. I found few items of news about them or indeed Asians or Muslims. So, the Mail reader is left to make his or her own mind up. Is it that good news stories are sent in by the readers and the Pakistani community does not send them in?

Probably the only occasion when Pakistani-Birmingham made it to the front page with more detailed coverage on the inside pages was to do with terror-related arrests of Pakistani young men. Of course, such news have to be covered but it should be balanced with a range of other material to enable the readers to form a rounded image of the Pakistani community.

Research conducted by London Metropolitan University has shown that Muslims are the new 'suspect' community and have taken over from the Irish who have held this position in the past. [69] Locally, James Arthur and colleagues have pointed out that "majority of Muslim students stated that Islam was misrepresented in the press." The Pew Report for 2008 also showed that opinions about Muslims across Europe were very negative. In view of this, if newspapers such as The Birmingham Mail do not provide an alternative viewpoint, people will go on believing that the negative image of the Muslim community is also true locally. As this concerns a large section of our city, any negative representation of Pakistanis or Muslims is a negative representation of Birmingham. To paraphrase Professor Carl Chin, "Media perceptions should be challenged and prejudices dispelled . . . we should not pander to prejudices and negative stereotypes about (Pakistani) Brummies" (Where the worlds meet) [70,] (hereinafter WTWM).

As a relevant aside, each month we have started to receive GEM Magazine which is delivered to households in South West Birmingham. So far it has profiled Rabbi Jacobs from Singer Hill Synagogue and Catherine Ogle, the Dean of Birmingham Cathedral. I look forward to similar profiles of religious leaders from the Pakistani community.

SECTION 3

SO, WHAT DO I THINK IS THE PROBLEM?

Nearly fifteen years ago, The Economist published an article on Birmingham which stated that:

> *"Birmingham's Asians are also making a cultural impact on Britain. The city has given birth to a new cuisine—the "balti" curry—which is now as much of a national staple as fish and chips"*[71]

It pointed out that Indians in the city were doing well because of their success in education; "(they) are already providing a new class of professionals and entrepreneurs, Pakistanis not so." It offered an explanation for their lack of success: "Since most of the Pakistanis were from a poor, rural background in Kashmir they have found it harder to find their feet." It then quoted Mohammed Younis, from the Birmingham's association of Pakistani professionals, saying that "the next generation will do much better . . . There is a huge emphasis on education and on making this our home." 12 years on, has Mr Younis' prediction come true?

It was Trevor Phillips, Chair of the Commission for Racial Equality, who had likened the National Health Service to a snow-capped mountain where the boss is almost always White[72]. As I look through the information I have gathered, I am led to the conclusion that we have our very own K2 here in Birmingham.

When organisations apply for funding or have other encounter with big bureaucracies, they are often asked for information which helps to establish their 'ethnicity'. If Birmingham plc was asked a similar set of questions, it would no doubt come out as a White organisation. Or looked on at a smaller scale, we could think of it as a White household which has a Pakistani cook and the driver with maybe one or two other non-White staff playing some support role.

We may like to think of organisations as 'just organisations'. But, if an organisation employs mainly White people, especially in all the key powerful roles and its culture is White and Western. Then, one should not be surprised if, from an ethnic minority point of view, such an organisation is seen as 'White' and, if it is seen to discriminate against Pakistanis or Muslims, as Islamophobic or Pakophobic. For many years, as I walked down Margaret Street offices of the Education Department, it was very clear what colour the organisation was; with all the officers, senior and junior, as White and the clerks and secretaries as Black or Asian. In my view, in Birmingham with its Pakistani and Muslim presence, such a situation is not sustainable.

Is racism to blame?

> *"On the front we are equal opportunity . . . but underneath it is all rubbish, racism is there . . .".* Avtar Johal

On arrival in Birmingham, the Pakistanis found themselves in a system which treated all communities the same, regardless of their circumstances and need. According to Sutcliffe and Smith, "the policy of the City Council towards coloured people was essentially to leave them alone." So, it was very much a survival of the fittest. The Pakistanis lost out to others. In the early days, this was to Whites but later on, they were in competition with other Asians or other ethnic minorities. In the world of employment they lost out to Indians who were and are l ahead in education. In employment, they also lost out to Black Caribbeans who, unlike earlier times, now were presumably seen to be both more suitable and acceptable given their cultural and religious background.

How things used to be!

Richmond School, Birmingham—discriminated against Pakistani teacher

On 27 February 1981 a tribunal found that the above school in Moseley Birmingham had discriminated against Miss

Najma Hafeez, a 24 year old Pakistani born teacher of English. According to my research, the previous year, Miss Hafeez was completing an Open University degree in English and Education. Richmond school was looking for teachers to teach English to Italian students on their summer courses. Miss Hafeez phoned the school and arranged a visit.

On arrival, according to her evidence, the Headteacher refused to interview her. He did not even look at her qualifications. He had said—he admitted it at the tribunal—the parents of these students want their children to be taught by English origin (meaning White) teachers. A few days later a White colleague of Miss Hafeez applied for the same job and was successful.

The case was decided in Miss Hafeez' favour. This was a landmark case because, according to the tribunal, it had far reaching implications for similar schools which are set up to teach foreign students.[73]

But, that was then. Surely, we don't have such situations in Birmingham now. We know race discrimination happened in the 1950s and 1960s before it was made illegal. What little racism happens now is only at the hands of the members of the British National Party. End of story.

I am mindful that words 'racism' and 'White privilege' can be sensitive subjects. We don't like to talk about them. An academic in a key role for promoting good relations amongst diverse communities once announced at a conference: "I don't like isms. I prefer adjectives such as multicultural and intercultural." Uncomfortable though it might be to talk about it, I believe that eradicating racism will take a little more than merely refusing to acknowledge its presence.

We certainly don't like to be told we are racist. In the Times Educational Supplement (11.5.2008), Mariane Cavalli, Principal, South Croydon College, was quoted as saying: "I can think of only one thing worse than being accused of being a racist and that is being accused of being a paedophile." Not nice at all! And yet, racism persists, real and tenacious. It has been likened to a monster which, like a hydra, again and again rears its ugly head. Part of the problem in its identification is that it can be practiced the same way and with the same intensity everywhere but vary with respect to each group chosen for disparagement[74] It has also been described as a virus that has mutated and evolved into a new form that is difficult to recognise and harder to combat[75].

The equality campaigner Ann Dummett, pointed out that people did not have to say they were racist for them to be so. The same was the case for institutions. She said that a racist institution had no need to put up a notice saying so; it could just use its operations to exclude certain people from jobs or only appoint them at lower grades with poorer pay and conditions. It was possible for an institution to be racially exclusive without saying so on a policy or memo. ". . . It is indeed perfectly possible for it to be racist in spite of written statements and exhortations to the contrary." In other words, racism could carry on in spite of statements such as:

WE ARE AN EQUAL OPPORTUNITIES EMPLOYER.

The myth of merit

Iris Marion Young has argued that some groups in society can suffer as a consequence of the *unconscious* assumptions of well meaning people which are expressed through ordinary interactions, in the media and other cultural stereotypes or how things are done in large organisations such as the City Council, health authority, and the financial sector; in other words, 'the normal processes of everyday life'(p41).[76]

Organisations which have an underrepresentation of particular groups often contend that they appoint 'the best person for the job' and 'they don't apply'. According to Iris Marion Young, the powerful who run our organisations establish the criteria for admitting others. They choose people who are like them ("instead of coming from the 'right' family, they went to the 'right' school); "persons who by nature or training exhibit the preferred behavioural and temperamental characteristics."

For Young, it is not just the current workers who should decide on criteria for new employees; those in the outside community especially the users of the service should also have a say. "Parents of children who attend a day-care centre, or consumer members of a health . . . organisation, should have a voice . . ." She goes onto say that representation of disadvantaged groups who experience cultural imperialism is crucial both in establishing job goals and in establishing evaluation procedures . . . to ensure that their particular experiences, culture, and values are not excluded or disadvantaged.

For Bhikhu Parekh, the concept of merit needs to be seen in a broader context of community benefit such as the appointment of Blacks and women as role models. "The collective need for a job becomes an important part of a Black or female applicant's *merit* and one of the bases of his or her right or even *entitlement* to it" (p271, original italics). Furthermore, Parekh argues that organisations do not exist in a vacuum and their purpose cannot be defined without reference to their obligations and responsibilities to the wider society. He questions the whole basis of 'qualifications for a job' or 'job-related qualifications'. He uses the concept of a 'good Doctor' to illustrate his point. We could equally talk of a 'good Headteacher', a 'good Police Officer' and so on. Instead of just focusing on his qualifications in order to admit him to a hospital, for Parekh, we could also ask that such a good doctor should posses certain qualities of character and temperament, compassion and a sense of social concern. "We could argue too that in a culturally and racially diverse society like ours, he should be able to relate to and inspire the confidence or people of different backgrounds, and be knowledgeable about their life-styles, stresses and strains, needs and approaches to health and disease. We could also argue that he should be able to appreciate that modern medicine is not the last word in scientific knowledge and that it can benefit from a dialogue with other medical traditions"[77], like faith healing, perhaps.

A universal approach to equality appears to have the same effect as not doing anything and leaving the situation to the vagaries of the free market. Communities are different; they are affected by discrimination differently. They have different capabilities too which determine the extent to which they are able to benefit from the opportunities on offer. What such a situation requires is a differentiated approach to provision of opportunities.

It is plausible that the exclusion of Pakistanis, talked about in DWP 360, could be happening here in Birmingham. We can see how the current culture of the organisations could reinforce itself by their leadership recruiting 'people like us' and excluding others because 'they will not fit in'. This is even more of a possibility in appointing for roles such as for governing bodies where rules are less clear.

Under the Race Relations Act 1976, the concept of 'Genuine Occupational Qualification' (GOQ) was introduced to address inequalities. The focus at the time was on exclusion of ethnic minorities generally or umbrella groups such as Asians. It was, as a result of this that I was able to obtain my first public sector job as a youth worker for

Birmingham City Council. This was as a part of the scheme the council had set up to recruit a team of six Black and two Asian youth workers. The work we were able to establish and develop during the two years we were in post would not have been possible without taking such a targeted policy approach.

Given the Pakistani underrepresentation in the city, is it time to establish a similar approach by accepting 'Pakistani' as a GOQ? This would enable us to do for Pakistanis what the City Council did, in 1978, for Blacks and Asians when it employed eight of us as trainee youth workers.

Stuart Hall has talked about institutions having their own cultures.[78] My experience over the years has told me that, within organisations, there are the formal policies and there is 'the way things are done'. It is in the latter where concepts such as 'we', 'other' 'fitting in' etc have a meaning. It is in this cultural context where some lose out. They either don't get in or, if they do, then they don't get on. They are excluded or exclude themselves through not playing the cultural games. And the kind of things I am talking about can be little: who goes for a drink or a football match with whom, who has seen whom over the weekend, who was Best Man at whose wedding; the list goes on. Ordinary things of the kind the philosopher Hannah Arendt spoke of when talking of the 'banality of evil'.[79] Within the context of the Holocaust, she had in mind people who were involved in routine activities such as showing up for work, typing a list, chairing a meeting, etc

We could talk of a 'banality of racism' whereby many decent law abiding liberal people who believe in equality for all end up doing little things or just go along with unjust and excluding practices of their colleagues and organisations and which collectively go to disadvantage particular ethnic or religious groups. Little things become big as explained here by the Macpherson Report:

> *"The collective failure of an organisation to provide an appropriate and professional service to people because of their colour, culture or ethnic origin which can be seen or detected in processes; attitudes and behaviour which amount to discrimination through unwitting prejudice, ignorance, thoughtlessness and racist stereotyping which disadvantages minority ethnic people."*[80]

It has also been argued that, although there is now less racism of the overt kind and more people are more positive about equal opportunities, there is still racism of a subtle kind. Even people who say they are not racist may actually be biased in subtle ways. Dovidio and Gaertner talk about 'aversive racism'. Their scientifically tested theory points out that aversive racists may not discriminate in all situations. They like to think of themselves, and like to be seen by others, as supporters of equality. So, they will not express their biases in a way which undermines this image. They will certainly not discriminate where the rules clearly dictate otherwise. Also, they may discriminate at times and in situations where they can justify it on grounds other than race e.g. poor performance, when all along it is race which is the cause of their behaviour. In this way they can insulate themselves from accusations, if made, and even believe that they are not racist.[81]

It is now clear that racism does not operate in a blanket way i.e. against all ethnic minorities. There is a hierarchy in operation. The government report DWP 360 pointed out that some employers have developed an 'aversion' to Pakistanis or Muslims generally. They did not wish to employ them because of their religious needs. They would rather employ people of their own (White) ethnic group or employ non-Pakistanis or non-Muslims. This has begun to give a clear message to the community. I came across one person saying in an article that, when applying for jobs, he pretends to be Indian rather than Pakistani. He finds this goes down better with employers. There is clearly a limit to how far one can go with such pretence. There is no hiding a beard or a headscarf.

We have learnt from history that groups and communities sometime start by being the 'outsiders', the 'other' or to borrow a word from Urdu, the 'pariahs'. But then they are welcomed as 'one of us'. This position has been held by the Jewish and the Irish communities before Black people. Which group does our society now see as not 'one of us', who may not fit in? In whose company do we, in polite society, feel uncomfortable? During the earlier stages of post-war migration it was all ethnic minorities who were the 'other'. As a city, we seem to have come to terms with the African Caribbean community and some Asians (i.e. Indian). I hope the same will happen one day with the Pakistani community.

According to Young, people claiming to be neutral still carry unconscious biases and prejudices against specially marked groups. It appears quite conceivable that the current 'Other', the Pakistanis, would end up losing out in such a situation. We know, for example, that candidates with the same qualifications can be rated differently in the recruitment process. Young suggests that "safeguards must be put on the bosses . . . to prevent their personal prejudices and preferences from influencing their decisions".

We have a tendency to see our liberal elite from Hegel's eyes—that they are the pinnacle of universal reason and are able to transcend, rise above, the world around them. Sadly, the reality is much closer to Marxist position, that is, that such people are very much a part of society and are not able to transcend it. They have their role in protecting their own and the interests of their social class. According to Gillborn, factors such as race, power and the wider system come together to disadvantage certain groups and by implication protect the existing privileged position of others.[82] He uses 'critical race theory' to explain that racism is endemic. It is extensive to such an extent that it is normal. The theory also challenges liberalism and its claims of neutrality, objectivity, meritocracy and colour-blindness. It suggests that these claims are nothing but camouflages and that formal equal opportunity laws are too limited in scope.

So, racism may not be overtly displayed though it will still be equally and sometime more brutal. It is likely to be practiced in spite of exhortations and public commitment to do the opposite. Also, if there is racism then it is likely to be practised more politely, with a smile given that its perpetrators are, in the words of Birmingham University's Dr Ian Grosvenor, likely to be 'decent' folk. After all, they are the people who run our organisations which are often the sites of 'institutional racism', which like aversive racism, is often indirect, maybe even unconscious but equally damaging to its victims. Both operate in more subtle and indirect ways. The perpetrators of both these kinds of racism are usually fully paid up egalitarians who truly aspire to be non-prejudiced. Grosvenor quotes the political activist and leader of the Indian Workers Association, Avtar Johal, saying that it was much easier fighting racism in the 1960s because it was overt; subtle racism was much more difficult to challenge.

Taking a conspiracy theory approach would lead me to ask different questions. While there may be a policy of equal opportunities, the practice at times may be a different matter. In a book on Winston Churchill, its author Richard Toye, talks about how a few weeks into World War 2, the great wartime leader wrote a note on employment of Indians or Colonial Natives in the Royal Navy. The note started quite positively: "There must be no discrimination on grounds of race or colour." But then he went onto say the opposite: "In practice much inconvenience would arise if this theoretical equality had many examples." Although, there are many examples of it, I have never come across it being described as "theoretical equality." Sir Winston then went onto explain what he actually meant, just in case some believer of justice misunderstood his intentions: "I cannot see any objections to Indians serving on HM ships where they are qualified and needed, or if their virtues so deserve rising to be Admirals of the Fleet." All well and good, you may think. But, then he takes much of it back by saying: "But not too many of them please." Not surprisingly, no Indian rose to become an Admiral of the Fleet in the Royal Navy during World War II. So, is that what we have for the Pakistanis; 'theoretical equality'; on paper it looks great but in reality, it does not amount to very much!

Thanks to all the campaigning of the Lawrence family, we had the Macpherson Report which for a brief period looked very hopeful. We even had a new law passed in the form of the Race Relations (Amendment) Act 2000. But then we went back to that colour-blind world again where either we did not mention equality or if we did then it was called diversity. It was much softer. We felt more comfortable with it. It was less threatening than equality. It had no association with inequality. It certainly helped us to forget unpleasant words such as racism. I know because I have worked, for many years, as a Diversity Consultant. We also came up with concepts such as Community Cohesion, as long as it was minority communities who changed their ways and stopped leading parallel lives.

It is now possible for organisations, led by decent liberals and with the correct policies and procedures, to have a diverse workforce and still not employ any Pakistanis or have the community involved in the governance. They can be seen to be 'equal opportunities employers' who can tick all the boxes of the equality legislation, pass inspections and achieve the kitemarks and yet discriminate against this very large community.

So, just because we come up with reports and policies which do not mention inequalities or racism, that does not mean the evil has gone away. Just because everyone has had their awareness raising training does not always mean that they have stopped practicing illegal discrimination. Sometimes, all it has done is to let people know how to stay on the right side of the law or out of employment tribunals.

Peacocks and penguins

In the *Racial Contract*, Charles Mills has talked about power spaces having a race. What race is the space currently in the upper half of the

City Council or the Police, Health or colleges and universities? How long before this too, like our wider society, becomes multiracial?

More generally, how is it for minorities within institutional settings that are overwhelmingly White and male? Do we know what it is like to be Black, Asian, Pakistani, Muslim—with or without a beard or headscarf—in the City Council or other large city organisations? Do they too, as peacocks, come under pressure to become like the penguins?[83]

Imagine you are in a meeting. You suddenly realise it's time for prayer. Would you have the courage to put your hand up to stop the proceedings for a little while so you could go and pray? It can take a lot of courage to do so. For example, I used to find it hard to excuse myself from some meeting at the college I worked at, saying: 'sorry folks, but I need to go and pick my child up from the nursery.'

Nirmal Puwar has explored what it means to be ethnic minority civil servants. For her, "it is important to stress that although the culture of the senior civil service is one whose standards are invisible to the degree that it is viewed as ordinary or objective, it is actually a culture whose standards are White, upper/middle-class and male."[84]

Her work leads me to wonder what it means for that small minority of Pakistanis who have reached a senior position. Do they feel as if they are impostors, the odd ones out? Do they feel out-of-place, over-exposed, too self-conscious, too different? Do people treat them as if they were in a junior role or are they, in the words of Frantz Fanon, infantalised? Do people question their competency or have higher standards of performance for them? Do they feel as if their starting line is a few steps behind their White colleagues? Do they carry the 'burden of representation' and have to expend more energy in order to not slip up and be noticed or feel that they have let their race down?

Puwar talks of 'soft things'—how you behave in a group, how you speak, how you dress—and their influence on who gets in to an organisation or who gets on. Is it likely that one may have 'Pakistani soft things' but not 'White soft things'? What are the likely implications? Given the 'assimilative pressures' over time, is one likely to get rid of the former and acquire the latter? How far should one go; is there a danger of going too far and becoming White? I would recommend everyone, especially the small number of ethnic minority elite to read Fanon's 'Black skins, White masks'. He spoke of (black) people losing their colour in order to acquire the necessary Whiteness so they can be accepted as 'normal' meaning White. Is there a similar process going on for Pakistanis or Muslims? No beards, no scarves or kameez-shalwar!

When I arrived in my job at Bilston College, there were very few, about 2%, Black and Asian staff. So, I was seen as an Asian and I saw myself as such. Fortunately, we were able to reach the position where we had over a quarter of the staff who were Black and Asian. Now, because there were so many of us, we were no longer Black and Asian but simply staff; lazy, hardworking, kind, nasty . . . This meant that we no longer carried the 'race burden', that is, when we slipped up on something we did not feel that our whole race would be seen as such. We knew, others knew, that just down the corridor, in the next department, there were Black and Asians who had not slipped up. Perhaps we can achieve a similar position in Birmingham.

A possible case of Paki bashing

Plenty has been written about this type of overt British racism, which involved White young men going out, as a leisure activity, to beat up Asians. Although, the term refers to Pakistanis, they were not its only victims. Also, it is important to point out here that, while Paki has been used in relation to Pakistanis, its usage pre-dates their arrival in the UK and even predates Pakistan. According to Akbar Ahmed, Jinnah was the first Pakistani and Mountbatten was the first Paki-basher[85]. However, he is at pains to point out that this is not to imply that Mountbatten was motivated by a racist hatred of Pakistanis like the young skinheads in the UK. "On the contrary, Mountbatten belonged to that generation of British who genuinely believed that it was time that Asians were given independence and treated with respect." However, Ahmed points out that his attitude towards the Pakistanis was very different. It was difficult not to conclude that he was hostile to (Pakistanis) and intent on 'bashing' them, if only in a metaphorical sense. As a result, at its birth, the new country of Pakistan had no money and few physical resources.

Whatever other causes of such bias there might have been for Mountbatten, the British historian, Niall Ferguson, offers one explanation: "He sided openly with the Congress Party against the Muslim League, a preference the more surprising (or perhaps not) given Lady Mountbatten's affair with the Congress leader Jawaharlal Nehru."[86] According to Ahmed "If Pakistan was treated with contempt by the

British, is it hardly surprising that the word 'Pakistani', itself truncated to 'Paki', became a term of abuse?.."

Professor Stuart Hall once talked about 'local forms of racism'. I believe that this is exactly the case, whereby the local form of this evil now has, as its focus, Pakistanis. So, following the Macpherson Report, perhaps we should label it 'institutional Paki-bashing. This, coupled with Islamophobia, given most Pakistanis are Muslims, could be the cause of the wholesale exclusion of Pakistanis in Birmingham, an idea which has some support of the then Department of Work and Pensions.

The key thing to remember is that there is a problem, whatever the reason. If it is racism that is at the heart of Pakistani exclusion in Birmingham then it will be a new kind of racism: differentiated, selective, unintentional, aversive and systemic. It maybe liberal and polite so is likely to come with a smile. Whatever the reason for the situation, we cannot ignore this state of affairs. If we wish for our city to succeed, then we have to get to the underlying causes of the problem and find a solution. Pakistanis are, after all the second largest ethnic group in the city. Their fortunes are intertwined with those of the city.

Networking; 'word of mouth' by another name!

During the 1980s, the then Commission for Racial Equality produced two videos to raise awareness about discrimination and equality. One was a general one which outlined the organisation's work while the other one was called CRE Employment. I used to use both in my equality work. With the new Race Relations Act 1976 as a backdrop, the video set out to explain how race discrimination works. One of the scenarios in the video went like this:

> A (White) guy meets his (White) friend in a pub for a drink and tells him there is a job opportunity. His friend shows interest so he says: "start Monday"

The message of the presentation was that this sort of practice should not happen because it worked against ethnic minorities.

After over 30 years work as an equality practitioner, it is my contention that word of mouth is still with us as a recruitment method. It may have become more sophisticated in how it is carried out, the levels of employment it affects may be fewer, it may now be used to exclude only some groups from opportunities and it may be known by other names but the method is still very much with us.

I believe 'word of mouth' recruitment practices disadvantage communities such as Pakistanis who don't always socialise and network with the right friends in the right places. They can also be over trusting of the system; it has been so for me for many years. There is a belief that you see a job advertised, you apply for it and then sit back for the system to work mechanistically. You think that the application will be assessed and a short list drawn up. And all of it will be fair and above board, especially when it comes to large and respectable employers in 21st century Birmingham. Of course, this is how the formal system will work so that it can be recorded and monitored. But, there may be a parallel process going on all the time especially for certain, very senior, jobs. Probably long before the job was even advertised, the organisation had someone in mind to be appointed to the vacancy.

According to the DWP 360, Muslims lose out in the world of networking particularly as much of it goes on in environments where alcohol is served. This limits the 'word-of-mouth' opportunities available. They contrasted this with the opportunities available to Hindus and Sikhs, who were more likely to be able to join their colleagues for drinks after work in pubs and bars. "Whilst this in itself is not a barrier to employment, it was raised by some of our experts as being relevant since it could present a barrier to career advancement and cohesion in the workplace. This in turn is likely to produce fewer career role models for the community, and perpetuate low aspirations."

I have experienced two lots of redundancies. After both of them, I was sent to talk to specialists for advice on my next steps. On one of the occasions, I was told that 80% of the jobs are filled through networking—"it's a case of who you know"—and word-of-mouth and 20% are advertised. The person proceeded to tell me, in our one-to-one session that the trouble was that 80% of the people think that jobs are filled through transparent processes. So that means that 80% of the people are in reality chasing 20% of the jobs. Coming from a country where who you are counts for everything, it is very easy for Pakistanis to be trusting of the system in the UK and think that practices are open and transparent. For many years, this was my attitude; thinking that I would just apply for a job and wait for the system to work according to merit. I am learning, slowly.

During the above training, I was also told that many employers rely on recruitment agencies. If the agency sends them one person who they like they may ask for a few more. They may still give the job to the first person but now "they can be seen to be practising equal opportunities." They can say they operated the merit principles and selected the best person from a range.

I was told by a fellow consultant who has worked in the public sector all his working life that he never relies on formal processes. "It's all who you know. I never advertise or chase work. I have made hundreds of thousands." I am not suggesting all the employment decisions when hiring consultants happen like this; merely that without the external scrutiny and accountability, it is possible.

In response to my Freedom of Information request on the employment of consultants, I have been told that for 2010-2011, the City Council spent £18,000,000. This was a reduction compared to previous year when the expenditure had been £23,000,000.

I had asked for an ethnic breakdown of the consultants, especially the number who were Pakistani. In response, I was informed they "do not monitor" the ethnicity of the consultants. So, it is possible that all the people employed were . . . . It is also possible that some who are employed in this way have inappropriate views on diversity or Pakistanis or Muslims. When employing regular employees, questions, albeit bland ones, are asked to weed out the racists and sexists. Does the same 'scrutiny' take place when consultants are employed? In relation to Pakistani involvement in this respect, it is possible that not many of them work in a freelance capacity. In the thirteen years I have been working as a consultant, I have not come across more than a few. Perhaps, the City Council and our Chamber of Commerce could help to build capacity as a Positive Action initiative.

In the hope of finding some effective practice in this respect, I contacted the National College of school leadership. During my time as Education Adviser, I worked with the organisation on a number of occasions. I was told that during 2011-12, the College's budget was £109, 200,000 and £39,000,000 was paid "directly to schools and academies. In response to my request, I was initially told, 6 September 2012, that the "number of employees of Pakistani heritage directly employed by (them) was 16 or 6.5%." I asked for the grades of these staff. They were not able to provide this information. More critically, on 2 November 2012, I was told the organisation had made a mistake. The 16.5% Pakistani staff should have "in fact referred to the total number of BME employees of the National College." I wonder how many of them are of Pakistani heritage!

Given that this also impacts on Birmingham schools, I also asked for equality information on the sub-contractors who use the £39,000,000. I was told the college does not hold this information. Does this not leave the field wide open for equality legislation to be flouted and methods such as 'networking' to be used in recruitment of delivery personnel?

Of course, ideally, we would wish for a different situation, one where business is done out in the open according to transparent rules which are applied fairly. Such a situation may never come. So the challenge for the Pakistani community is to face the reality as it is, head-on.

Someone pointed out that 'word of mouth' happens within the Pakistani community too, for example, with jobs in the taxi or restaurant trades. While there is a world of difference between the two situations—you can earn more in a day as a top management consultant than you will in a month of driving people around the city or waiting at tables—it does help to explain the situation. So, if I can be bold as to offer some advice to the community: let's get real; this is how business is done in the world that surrounds us. The sooner we accept that, the sooner we will start to find solutions that do not compromise cultural and religious sensibilities.

PARALLEL LIVING IN BIRMINGHAM

"The (Pakistani) community remains largely insular and disconnected from other communities in the city. Given the size of the community and its impact on the city, it is vital to build cross community relationships, assume leadership roles in Birmingham to integrate and enhance community cohesion." Pakistani Network

"Cohesion is at the very centre of our city, it is the heartbeat of our organism. We have to find a way of making us all feel that we belong, whether we have lived here all of our lives or just recently arrived. It's not just about ensuring that newer communities have a stake; it's about making sure that we all see this as our home regardless of age, gender, faith or culture. We are all Brummies." (WTWM)—Councillor Waseem Zafar,

There is a book, 'Parallel Lives', by Phyllis Rose. It is about marriages of famous people such as John Ruskin, JS Mill and Charles Dickens. It described how they and their wives lived a separate and parallel existence.

Just as in these marriages, in multicultural societies such as ours, there are different communities existing side by side, leading their own lives on their own terms; also for good reason. When there was rioting in the Northern Towns of England, the government commissioned a number of reports. One of these, by Ted Cantle, caused a rebirth of the phrase 'Parallel Lives'. Sadly, often when the phrase is used, it is implied or stated explicitly that it is the minority communities such as the Pakistanis who are the guilty party and are, therefore, the ones who were leading parallel lives, keeping themselves apart from the rest of society. Little has been said of White people who keep themselves to their own kind or who have created the conditions which encourage separate existence. Just as it would have been wrong when discussing marital lives to blame the situation on one party, so it is when discussing community relations. As they say 'it takes two to . . . .'.

As a result of what was done by our policy makers in the 1950s, our different ethnic communities have come to develop separately in places such as Birmingham; a sort of South African Bantustans. It has been pointed out such separation is the reason we have little ethnic conflict. Sadly, little appears to have been done by the city to create understanding between the communities.

In my work in Birmingham, I have come across a number of examples which point to a problem of racial prejudice, a fear of the Other. This has to be addressed before our efforts to promote positive social relations will bear fruit. One outer ring school told me of their Whiteparents' refusal to go to Star City cinema complex in Nechells "because there are too many Pakis there." Here, I had intervened to prevent a 10 year old White boy being arrested for hate crime; he had used the 'N' word with a Black mate, thinking it a normal word. Afterwards, the Headteacher had emailed to say if the arrest had gone ahead, it would have put community cohesion back at least ten years.

During another equality assignment, the young residents of a city-wide housing organisation told me how football matches between their different sites would not work because of their reluctance to travel to a 'foreign area'. In my view, the 'Longbridge Mosque' incident arose out of such a fear of the 'Other'.

At the time of the 'northern riots' mentioned above, I know we as a city were pleased that such discord had not surfaced in our communities. Here, it is worth pointing out that some of the White trouble-makers, up-north, were our own citizens. I recall reading a report in The Observer newspaper at the time about eleven (others have said it was thirteen)[87] people appearing in front of Oldham magistrates and six of them had given their addresses in Bromford and Erdington. I have nieces and nephews living in both these areas, possibly with 'the six' as neighbours.

Sadly, from time to time professionals too are a part of the problem in such situations. During my research on the educational achievement of the White working class in Birmingham, I recall suggesting to the Headteacher of an Outer Ring school that he should consider twinning his mainly White school. Before I had the chance of saying who with, he said, "as long as we don't have to link up with one of those schools in Saltley or Sparkhill." That shut me up for that is exactly what I had in mind; thinking that both sets of school communities would equally benefit from such a relationship.

According to the Coalition Government, integration can be undermined and even reversed by a range of factors, for example "if groups within the local community work and socialise separately, if some sections of the local community face particular deprivation and adverse competition, or if extremist groups try to provoke tensions."

Parallel Worlds in Moseley

After a year's break, I decided to have another go at stewarding at the Moseley Folk festival. Where else can you be useful to your community, meet friends and neighbours and experience some excellent music as a part of the bargain? And all this for free when you're a steward. Not bad at all!

By Sunday, I had done my two shifts of duty so I could just enjoy the programme. But then I remembered that I had wanted to go to the Eid Mela taking place the same afternoon. So I decided to take a detour and first pop down to Canon Hill Park with thousands of other local people. I then managed to get to Moseley Park just in time for one of my favourite acts from two years ago, Scott Matthews.

Although the two events were taking place in different parts of our community, they seemed to be worlds apart.

Having spent many years locally, I have become used to feeling at home in a multiracial environment. So, what struck me above all was that the crowd at the mela were almost wholly Asian. There was a complete lack of any White faces with the exception of a few women who had married out of their community and, of course, some of the people who were staffing the display from organisations such as HSBC, Ford and Aston Villa Football Club who were there as a part of their outreach programme. And then later, at the folk festival, the crowd was slightly more multi-racial, predominantly White, with the occasional Black or Asian face.

It reminded me of the phrase 'parallel lives' coined after the 90s riots in a number of northern towns. At the time, it appeared to imply that it was the Pakistani community who was the guilty party. I wasn't sure who was to blame or indeed whether there was anything wrong with communities participating in distinct cultural events.

Surely, the main point is that people are free to choose what they want to do, on their Sunday afternoon. It could be having a pint of Mad Goose and listening to some up and coming folk artist with their friends and family or, a couple of hundred yards down the road, listening to Pakistani music also with friends and family but without the ale.

I did wonder, however, whether we will come to a time when we will stop having separate cultural events; perhaps a better option would be for both the events, and others like them, to have a more diverse participant experiencing difference at close quarters and learning about and from it.

We know an essential pre-condition of cohesion is trust. We also know that to engender such trust, there has to be meaningful contact; mere geographical closeness is not enough as we have learnt in Birmingham Hodge Hill. The constituency is made up of four wards, with a good level of ethnic diversity, as follows:

Hodge Hill	14%	Shard End	8%
Washwood Heath	57%	Bordesley Green	71%

According to WTWM, in spite of the ethnic diversity, there is a low level of trust in the area, the lowest for Birmingham at 14.5%. It would appear that, this is one place where more needs to be done before we can say that we are truly a 'we' city.

David Goodhart has reminded us that lack of contact between ethnic groups is a recipe for low trust and prejudice.[88] And we know that one of the preconditions of trust within societies is equality[89], a fact acknowledged by Councillor Zafar: "I really do feel that addressing the inequality gaps . . . . will go a long way towards ensuring that Birmingham is a socially cohesive city"(WTWM). At our meeting with Dr Ally, the City Council's Head of Equalities, he had also said: "you can't address cohesion if you don't address inequalities." The sooner we set out to achieve this and remove the barriers of exclusion and racism for the Pakistani community, the better it will be for all of us.

As my article above points out, parallel living involves more than one community; blaming ethnic minorities for it, as is often the case, is neither productive nor helpful. We need a city-wide strategy to address this problem. Also, in discussion of cohesion, very little attention has been paid to indifference[90]. In our multicultural context, it would be foolish to mistake what has been described as 'uncommunity[91]' as an expression of a tolerant Birmingham.

The Feast is a type of initiative that we need more of in the city. It brings together teenagers of different faiths to build friendships, explore faith and change lives. They start by developing relationships with the young people and then invite them to events where they can meet others from their own and other communities.[92] The initiative was founded by Dr Andrew Smith who is currently the Bishop of Birmingham's Director of Interfaith Relations. Dr Smith has recently been nominated by The Muslim News for "Excellence in championing a Muslim cause."[93]

Near Neighbour is another organisation which offers an antidote to separate communities. It involves "bringing people together who are near neighbours in communities that are diverse, so they can get to know each other better, build relationships as people and collaborate together on initiatives that improve the local community they live in." It encourages social interaction and encourages people "to come together for initiatives that improve their local neighbourhood", as illustrated by the video of the 'Saturday Stop-by' project run by the Islamic Society of Britain.[94]

The above initiatives provide much needed opportunity for people to come together to explore their multiple identities; their differences as well as their commonalities. The initiatives offer much potential for development. In the post-Apartheid South Africa it has been found that intergroup contact reduces various types of prejudice, and it is particularly effective when it unfolds under favourable conditions of equality, cooperation, and institutional support. "There is an emerging consensus that the promotion of intergroup contact should be adopted as a universal ideal."[95]

Another model we could look to is the 'One America' programme, on race and reconciliation, which was initiated by President Bill Clinton[96]. Could we initiate a One-Birmingham programme, with a series of city-wide conversations between our many different communities? For Jonathan Sacks[97], conversation is a disciplined act of communicating and listening. It's a process of showing respect, "of paying attention to the other, of conferring value on his or her opinions even though they are not mine." In such a situation, "neither side loses and both are changed, because they now know what reality looks like from a different perspective."

The historian and sociologist Stuart Hall said that we should address the sense of alienation of White working class, "who have to be won over to a new conception of themselves . . . ." In many ways, we could all do with such help to get in touch with our developing selves as Brummies. A conversation on the subject would certainly help.

Forgiveness and reconciliation as pre-conditions of cohesion

Much of the focus for cohesion has been on vertical relationships i.e. between White and ethnic minorities, mainly Pakistanis. There has been little discussion of horizontal cohesion, that is, between the different minority communities. For us the troubles in Lozells a few years ago between the Asian and African Caribbean communities was a reminder of when things can go wrong. The conflict began with a rumour spread by the newspaper of one ethnic group that men from the other ethnic group had raped one its women. The newspaper was reprimanded by the Press Complaints Commission for its irresponsible conduct. Untold damage was done during the troubles to property and community relations including killing of an innocent young man, by people for whom he belonged to the opposing side.

In my meeting, the City Council's Head of Equalities had spoken of "inter-ethnic racisms" in Birmingham. From my work with schools, I have been told that, amongst ethnic minorities, it is not uncommon for parents in one community to refuse to send their children to a school which has too many of another minority.

Drawing on the personal; I grew up in Pakistan of the 1950s and 1960s. I heard stories of Partition and our country's relationship with India. It was clear to me that India was an enemy country. Later, the same was to happen in relation to the new country of Bangladesh. But, then coming to Birmingham meant the citizens of these 'enemy' countries were now my neighbours. I had to work through what this meant for my relationship with them.

We are told (in WTWM) that there are now some 187 nationalities living in our city. Some of them would have similar histories of conflict. They are also likely to face the challenge of living as city-neighbours with people who they might have, until recently, seen as the enemy. Is it time we facilitated for such communities to put their past behind and look ahead to a new and different future!

Cohesion is like a marriage; communities coming together. Now that we want a not just geographical but a social living together as an integrated community we need to rethink how we interact with each other. There is no pretending the past did not happen. It did and it has left a nasty taste behind for some. If we are to move on into a different future, we have to deal with that past.

I am glad that we have started to talk of Brummie as an identity. But, I believe we are some steps away from reaching this particular destination. It's not simply a question of re-labelling the tin; we have to look at what's inside too. Perhaps, it could form part of the 'One Birmingham' conversation.

According to Sacks, the liberal virtues of tolerance, compromise, reason "cannot be preached to those who are mad with fear or mad with vengeance." We live in a world where groups are still in conflict over something that may or may not have happened hundreds of years ago. Therefore, it is foolish to imagine that memories of a conflict that happened in the 1990s, 1970s, even in the 1940s, have been erased for communities who have made our city their home.

For Sacks, forgiveness is a counterintuitive idea. "In a world without forgiveness, evil begets evil, harm generates harm . . . It represents a decision not to do what instinct and passion urge us to do. It answers hate with a refusal to hate, animosity with generosity." And, if we are not destined to replay the grievances of yesterday, it is necessary "to live with the past without being held captive by the past." We have to forgive each other for our actions or the actions of our ancestors in the hope of creating a city community at peace with itself and where the different peoples trust each other and respect each other. Only then will we live as one. Not separate parts but interlinked and interdependent. A community where your origins and your religious beliefs will not be a barrier to you becoming a part of the city community. Forgiveness—of self, others as well as by others—is also a means of liberation from shame.

The Nishkam Centre was the venue for an interfaith conference on the topic of 'Forgiveness' organized by the Universal Peace Federation. It was the first such conference held in Birmingham.[98]Following Sacks' advice, we need to explore the concept further in order to reconcile the different pasts. This is not something just for others like post-apartheid South African, to mention just one society where they have gone beyond the mere surface in the hope of creating a more robust society[99]. Nearer home, with reference to Northern Ireland, it has been said that "even after a conflict has formally ended, there is still a need for post-conflict reconciliation and the building of mutual forgiveness and trust between communities[100]. Here they have used the concept of forgiveness with young people who were not themselves involved in conflicts but have only heard about them from parents. This has implications for our city where there are many young people who have similarly 'experienced' conflicts through their parents' stories.

A CONVERSATION WITH TAHIR ABBAS

"One scenario might be that we have Birmingham with a Black majority city but the institutions are still effectively White run. So you could have a situation like South Africa, where even though it's a Black majority city, the majority of citizens are receiving services that still don't meet their needs . . . a recipe for tension . . . . You'd expect resistance, tension and polarisation between those who are recipients and those who are dispensing the services"—Bruce Gill

In 1996, Bradford had set up a commission to look into its community relations. M Taj who had been its member decided to write a supplementary report: A 'Can Do' City. Here, Taj had stated:

- The "Muslim' communities are notoriously bad at representing their own interest. Factionalism is rife—there is an adage that if you have 'two Pakistanis in a room you'll have three organisations'. The multiplicity of community, religious and cultural organisations prevents the communities having a coherent and forceful voice about their own most pressing interest. It is also a besetting sin of leading community figures wanting to be 'big fish in small ponds' rather than mere contributors to a more unified representation.
- The sub-ordinate role of women in the 'Muslim' communities presents a real problem. A problem . . . of a community that is not allowing the full development of half its potential economic and intellectual strength

But that was Bradford, we are Birmingham. I wonder how much of what he said applies to My Hometown.

126

When I set out on this project, I had wanted to hold structured conversations with key members of the Birmingham Pakistani community. Sadly, given that I could not get any funding for the work, that was not possible. So, it's become a one-way conversation. The only exception has been this email exchange with Abbas. I thought I would turn to him for his views on the situation. His assessment was, after all, one of the reasons why I set out on this project. Here is our email exchange, conducted 23-24 July 2012:

Karamat: Congratulations on your new appointment. I continue with my research into Pakistani boys' education and about Pakistanis generally within Birmingham

Tahir: Many thanks indeed—good luck with your on-going research. If I can help in any way, please do let me know. Best Wishes

Karamat: The more I look at the situation of the Pakistani community in Birmingham, the more convinced I am of their exclusion and marginalisation. As someone who knows the city well, what is your view?

Tahir: The situation is bad and getting worse. You're being polite. Exclusion and marginalisation are lighter terms for something deeper. It's basically racism—and always has been—no matter how it is dressed up around values, identity, culture and even cohesion—it is deep-seated, systematic and pervasive—and because it is historically embedded into every aspect of economy and society, it will get worse as Blightly wallows in austerity, for probably a generation . . . the young, who are more than half of all Pakistanis (under 25) have no real future—the city has systematically failed to plan for an ethnic minority majority population—I was screaming this stuff out back in 2003/4 onwards . . . I hate to say it, as I don't want to big up myself too much, I came out in public to say these things—but did anyone listen? Was I proved right?

Of course, the Pakistanis do not help themselves—the elders play Pakistani politics, which is basically feudalistic—then the mosques and imams are out of touch—and then the women are excluded from the public sphere in general—but the issue is direction—Pakistanis end up doing this because they are squeezed in this direction—professional Pakistanis find alternative means to engage, but not without limitation of course. All Pakistanis are 'exposed' in the current period . . .

In Turkey, there is a great deal of 'izzat' towards Pakistanis for basically what the territory did for Turkish independent movements in the 1930s. In the UK, they still say 'Paki Go Home', as the APL and NF did in the 70s—I still remember those walls in our neighbourhood (Small Heath, Byron Road) in the late 1970s daubed with racist graffiti—when you get to my age you realise pretty quickly that things don't really change, nor do people—real change takes a very long time, if at all—often, we just find another way of doing the same thing—the same thing that has been going on for centuries . . .

> *Karamat*: I am hoping to write a long note about this subject in the hope of starting a discussion in the city amongst both Pakistanis as well as others. Is it ok to quote your comments?
>
> *Tahir*: I think I just fired off a bit of a rant—yes, happy to help, but it would be good if I could expand the details—please let me see any final version before you send it out—not that I fear being misquoted :) but I just want to ensure it is pitched at the right level to make the necessary impact. Good luck—happy to help (edited by Abbas 2 February 2013)

In another conversation, I was asked to not forget Pakistani women and the role they should be playing in the city. The cover picture was in some ways my response, of a Birmingham future yet to come. Dr Maliha Lodhi was the first woman in Asia to edit a national daily newspaper and was awarded the Hilal-i-Imtiaz Presidential Award for Public Service. She was twice appointed as Pakistani Ambassador to the United States (1994-1997 and 1999-2002). She was her country's High Commissioner to the UK, 2003-2008. During her time here, in an interview cited earlier, she pleaded that Pakistani women should be treated as equal partners and not 'hidden away' in the family home.

Here in Birmingham, we had the first female Pakistani councillors, Najma Hafeez and then Salma Yaqoob, who both helped to challenge their own and the wider community's stereotypes. But then it took a long time before we saw other Pakistani women councillors as we did last year with the election of three in the East of the city. Let's hope for a few more very soon as well as women playing their fullest role elsewhere in the city.

Our post-war Birmingham history would tell us that we have come a long way. There was a time when we had a colour bar in jobs, housing, education and leisure outlets. Its aim was to exclude all ethnic minorities, not just Pakistanis. There were some amongst our city's political elite who wanted our communities to 'go back home':

> ". . . It was the political elite who, with officers, took policy decisions. These decisions, in turn, served to define and constrain the opportunities available to Birmingham's Black population. These policy decisions were responsible for the reproduction of racism and inequality in Birmingham" (Grosvenor, p114)

So compared to those days, we have made tremendous progress. But, we still have some way to go as far as Pakistanis are concerned.

In March 1976, Philip Jones told us in 'Colored Minorities in Birmingham' (Annals of the Assn of American Geographers) that West Indians were a *racial minority* while Indians and Pakistanis were an *ethnic* group as well and whose "traditions . . . are a condition of existence, a crucial source of identity and pride, the constituent bonds of loyalty, respect, and obligation and an indispensable base for all interactions."

Fifteen years later, we had Stuart Hall draw attention to the inadequacy of the racial term 'Black'—to describe all ethnic minorities—and, in particular it's silencing of Asians:

> "Because though Asian people could identify, politically, in the struggle against racism, when they came to using their own culture as the resource of resistance, when they wanted to write out of their own experience and reflect on their own position, when they wanted to create, they naturally created within the histories of the languages, the cultural tradition."[101]

Later, Tariq Modood made a similar point and spoke of anti-Asian cultural antipathy.[102] He quoted John Rex in saying that amongst social scientists and policy makers, the structure of the various Asian communities and the problems which Asians faced had been "seriously misunderstood because of the focus on the disadvantages suffered by, and discrimination against, Blacks"[103].

Such challenge remained isolated. It was not given any support from the numerous equality practitioners. Consequently, little attention was paid to the needs of the Pakistani community especially that which centred on the cultural (as opposed to racial) discrimination and may explain their current predicament. It would appear that there is a hierarchy of communities in our city—White, Black, Indian, and Pakistani—with ethnic groups experiencing inequalities unequally. Therefore, any response to the problem will also need to be differentiated.

In spite of coming from a very disadvantaged background, Pakistanis have made tremendous success of themselves. However, they have been playing catch up ever since.

When I set out on this project, it was to get 'under the skin' of the views expressed by Abbas and Pakistani Community Development Network. All the evidence I have gathered leads me to agree with both of them. With reference to the reports from the Lawrence Commission and Citizens Alliance, I would say that as far as Pakistani-Birmingham is concerned 'things are not working' and there is a very serious 'cause for concern'.

To paraphrase an article on the Chamberlain Forum website: "what links a taxi driver in Birmingham with an investment banker . . . ?" [104] the answer would be 'very little'. The barriers between them are very strong indeed with the shutter well and truly closed. The article goes onto point out that "a relatively small group of people—perhaps 500 in total—are directly involved in making strategic decisions about the future of the city and its people." For me, it raises the obvious question: 'how many of them are Pakistanis? We talk of 'reflective' workforces. So that should be around 50 Pakistanis. I also wonder how many Pakistanis are there just outside the 500-group; being trained and developed to step into the top positions as the Pakistani presence in the city increases.

The article points out that "between ten and fifty thousand people in Birmingham are two steps from power . . . The majority of citizens are three steps from power." Is this where the Pakistanis are, I wonder? Or are they amongst the "large minority . . . . who are excluded: there are more than three degrees of separation between them and the people making the decisions affecting them?"

Of course we no longer have signs such as the ones we were used to seeing in the 1950s and 1960s which were designed to keep out the Irish and the Blacks. It would be illegal for a start. But surely the organisations which employ few or no Pakistanis, while may not have a 'Pakistanis Keep Out' banner outside their building, are giving the same message.

Or is it the problem to do with the Pakistani community itself? Maybe they are just happy to drive taxis and wait at tables in cheap balti restaurants? But whatever the reason for Pakistani exclusion and underrepresentation from key organisations of the city, surely it cannot be good for the city's cohesion? In my view, we should aim for a situation where the Pakistani community is integrated in all aspects of our city—as clients and service providers, at different levels of employment within organisations and on governing bodies, in proportion to their presence in the city.

Of course, if they are not up to the job, then that is another matter altogether. Except that would then raise questions about our education system, our schools, our second chance institutions like colleges and our universities, given most Pakistanis were born here and have been through the education system. Do we know what the explanation is for Pakistani graduates doing menial jobs?

People, who have scant knowledge of the city, have said that we are at peace with our diversity. I would say, we are so in part. We are comfortable with Black people. With Asians we are OK as long as they are Indians, with a few Pakistanis thrown in for good measure. As for Pakistanis generally, we need to do much more work before we can say 'job done'.

We have made tremendous progress in our society on race equality but only for some social groups. We know Indians and Chinese do very well in education and consequently in the rest of life. We now know that here in Birmingham, Bangladeshi pupils especially boys who used to underachieve have begun to do much better. Long may it continue. We still have a problem in the city as far as African Caribbean educational achievement goes, again of boys. Something has to be done about this.

We have also succeeded in the employment of African Caribbean people across the city. This is something we should celebrate. Here is a group of people who were once the pariahs of our society but now we are happy to work alongside them and in some cases where they are actually the bosses. But that still leaves the Pakistanis who continue to be excluded from the mainstream of our society. All the data points to employers, with a few exceptions, denying them the opportunities on offer. While being the largest non-White group in our city since 1991, they continue to be noticeable by their absence across the city's employers.

In a pamphlet published over a quarter of century ago, Danielle Jolly from Warwick University had said: "This paper has shown that Muslims cannot be overlooked in Birmingham in 1986."[105] In my view, much still remains to be done, in 2013, for the largest of the Muslim communities, the Pakistanis.

Bruce Gill[106], the then Council's Head of Equalities, had presented two scenarios: one given above, and the other, his (and my) preferred option:

> *"Or you could have . . . . a Black majority city (where) we will have representations in the highest echelons of responsibility, not just in the City Council, I'm talking about health, the police, etc and the lessons have been heeded and the commitment is producing services which meet the needs of our people. I'm optimistic and I believe that, in a city like Birmingham, that's the direction in which we will wish to move and in which we will move."*

Of course, it is now more likely to be a case of Asian majority, mainly Pakistani, or Muslim majority Birmingham. My worry is that if nothing is done to change things, we will end up having British Raj all over again. Except, this time it would be in our city, with a mainly Asian population being governed (ruled!) by White people, what has been called 'internal colonialism.'[107] The term 'tolerant imperialism'[108] is also relevant here. This was how JS Mill, the "most influential English-speaking philosopher of the nineteenth century" defended the British Raj in India. The trouble was that his position was somewhat compromised because, for roughly half his life he was a loyal employee of the East India Company which had laid the foundations for the British presence in the region.

PAKISTANIS ARE DIFFERENT

Dr Idraneel Sircar and Dr Jyoti Saraswati have drawn attention to the diversity within the Asian community. Researching a London community, they have said that there were two strands of the British Asian experience. One was the affluent group who were in White collar professional jobs and who were leading comfortable lives. They were passing the advantages to their children. While the second group were the poor, in manual jobs (if they had any), living in disadvantaged inner city areas and whose children followed in their footsteps with similar career trajectories.

Sircar and Saraswati said that the term 'British Asian' did capture the diversity that exists within the community in terms of ethnicity, religion, social class, migration history, or other factors. They also reminded us that the term 'Asian' had little meaning for the community itself. [109]

I mentioned to a fellow Pakistani Brummie about my research into educational achievement of Pakistani boys. I shared with him my hunch that it was probably Kashmiris Pakistanis who were underachieving. He said the Pathan boys were equally underachieving. He believed they lacked appropriate role models. This reminded me of a conversation with another Brummie Pakistani. He had said that Pakistanis in Small Heath were different from the Pakistanis in Alum Rock. In due course, this all needs unpicking instead of talking simply of Pakistanis as if they were all the same.

It has been pointed out that racial inequality does not affect all ethnic minorities in the same way. "Caribbean, Black Africans, Indians, Chinese and others, and White migrants all obtained upward mobility relative to White non-migrants . . . . However, the picture for the Pakistanis is the reverse."[110] Not only do the Pakistanis have a disadvantaging social class origins, education does not seem to make a difference for them. "Not even higher levels of qualifications can bring them the same occupational rewards as their White counterparts; whereas for other groups the route to their greater levels of upward mobility is through education." Qualifications "seems to be a way for achieving parity, for compensating for past discrimination and for building success for some groups" but not for Pakistanis (and Bangladeshis). For them, "ethnic group effects outweigh any such achievements."

Others have also focused on how Pakistanis are different. I refer to two such reports; both include Bangladeshis, given the similarities between the two communities. The first is DWP 360. This concluded that "ethnic penalty is most severe for Pakistani and Bangladeshi men and women."

Motherhood as an identity

DWP 360 pointed out that some Pakistani women positively chose to place family life before anything else and this was also true for women with higher levels of qualifications. It advised that women who placed family before career should not be seen as having a 'problem' or being 'victims'. It found that such women saw it as their responsibility to teach their children the culture, language and the religion and many of them considered work which clashed with their family responsibilities as unsuitable such as that which involved shift-work and travel. It is worth pointing out that even in our post-feminist world, such counter-cultural identities are also prevalent amongst some practising Christian communities.

Pakistanis (and Bangladeshis) have been identified as 'different' by others too[111], while cautioning against the dangers of generalisations. We have been reminded that it is wrong to think of the communities as 'static', as changes are taking place within them.

The community tends to marry early, has higher rates of marriage and has more transnational spouses. There is some fall in marriage rates especially amongst the UK born Pakistanis. Rising education is also a possible factor here. There is some evidence to show that marriage with spouse from Pakistan is more common amongst the UK born Pakistanis and those who came here as children. This adds an additional dimension to the 'difference' for the community.

Pakistanis have a higher rate of fertility. The Office for National Statistics showed that, in 2001, the total fertility rate for mothers born in the UK was 1.6, 2.3 for mothers born in India, 3.9 for mothers born in Bangladesh and 4.7 for mothers born in Pakistan.

In terms of female employment, in 2006, the rate for Pakistani women was 20% compared to 60% for other ethnic groups. Although the rate has been rising, the same was true for other ethnic groups. The Equalities Review pointed out that the gap will never be eliminated. However, the rate varies; it was 45% for UK born Pakistani women and 18% for those born in Pakistan. Change in this respect is also said to be taking place in the Pakistani community where there are no dependent children.

As elsewhere, the community has been described as overwhelmingly Muslim and like all Asian communities, "extremely religious." Islam has been shown to have a much higher retention rate—"almost 90% of those who were brought up Muslim continue to practice their faith." The move to become less religious is "less marked for Muslims than for those of other faiths." Also, that the "overwhelming majority of Pakistanis . . . will describe themselves as Muslims for generations to come and a majority will continue to practice their faith." Overall, it has been pointed out Muslims were different in the ways expected but that the differences were declining. The sooner we begin to accommodate the differences the better will be for our future.

DWP 360 pointed out that if children do well, they may enter the professions (doctors, lawyers or accountants). They will be encouraged to go into these careers. But, if they do not reach the necessary levels of academic achievement, then they go onto menial jobs. They pointed to a lack of role models within the Pakistani community who can help to widen aspirations and encourage young people to consider options "outside these two traditional polarised career paths." How many plumbers do we have who are Pakistani? It's a skilled job that pays well. The report also pointed out that there was a lack of Asian (Pakistani!) role models in senior management in both the public and private sector. "This may be preventing young Pakistanis . . . from aspiring to a wider range of careers."

As pointed out elsewhere, in order to understand the Pakistani community one needs to have a good comprehension of the ethnic penalty they face, described as the 'Pakistani effect'.[112]

For the Pakistanis, there can at times be a conflict with the individualist culture of the West. It's a people who, for example, place a much greater emphasis on family. This has to be considered by employers when their employees may need to attend to family obligations such as attending funerals.

The Pakistanis in the main are a polite and civilised community. They just get on with life and always have. Even the person who has little, will, when asked, is likely to say they are fine; they are managing. The community is generally very good at making do with the little resources they have. However, in my view, the community does not help itself; it does not complain enough. The American civil rights leader, Jesse Jackson once said that the worse thing that can happen to a disadvantaged community is when it thinks its situation is normal. Has this happened to the Pakistani community? Does the community think it is normal and natural that its members do the menial jobs instead of those that pay tens of thousands more!

Pakistani youth don't riot as a general rule. In spite of its large presence and having a youthful community, during the Birmingham riots last year, there were very few of its youth on the streets. This was also the time when we as a city had the inspirational leadership of Tariq Jahan who, having lost a son and two nephews, still had the moral stature to calm the situation. It is not worth contemplating what might have happened if he had not. During the writing of the book, I had a dream where Mr Jahan was the answer to a question on a cereal packet. In the real world what he did may be more appropriate for text books

The close knit nature of the community has been an asset. It provided the community the safety and security in the face of a hostile world during its early days. But is it something that is holding the community back? When I go to schools to talk to young Pakistanis I wonder whether their aspirations have been lowered by what they see each and every day of their existence. Some of them seem to get excited at the prospect of earning a few hundred pounds each week not realising that there are people who earn the same and even more in a day.

Part of the problem may lie in the fact that the Pakistani community in Birmingham is not one cohesive community, but many smaller communities which are organised according to the region of Pakistan they come from. Furthermore, the larger ones, like the Kashmiris, are at times having to give their time and energy to the as-yet-unresolved issue of their independence of their disputed country. This also sets them apart from the rest of Pakistanis. Then there are divisions of biraderi or family, region and political party membership (including of numerous Pakistani parties). The community continues to expend its energies on politics of Pakistan instead of focusing its energies here. At times, its leaders are too busy attending political rallies about 'back home' or entertaining leaders who should be in Islamabad instead.

Teenage parenthood

According to a government briefing on teenage pregnancy, "for some of the young people in the study particularly those of Muslim faith, early parenthood within marriage is not viewed negatively or stigmatised. Policies that focus on reduction of teenage parenthood need to acknowledge the differing perspectives on early parenthood within some cultural groups where there may be extensive family support for teenage parents who are usually married."[113]

Muslim young parents placed a high value on motherhood and children, as their social norms concerning younger marriage and parenthood differed from those in the wider community. "Therefore, a focus by public agencies, such as the Teenage Pregnancy Unit, on reduction of teenage pregnancy per se has little meaning for communities in which it is a 'cause for celebration'." Such a situation also points to the role of second-chance organisations such as FE colleges and universities to help meet the needs of adults who wish to study after having children.

"I have 10 GCSEs and 2 AS levels. Um, like I said um, I'm hoping to do midwifery in three years time or in two and a half years, when he goes to nursery." (Young mother of Muslim faith)

Given that the dimensions of early parenthood (for Pakistanis) are very distinct from those factors that impact upon the experience of early parenthood in the mainstream society, it has been recommended that a much larger and in-depth research programme is undertaken. I cannot think of a place where the need for such research is greater than in Birmingham.

A related area that will require similar attention is that of sex education in schools. Views on this vary within the Pakistani community as they do in other faith-based communities. A few years ago the issue was debated within the Muslim Parliament. Even parents who are happy for their children to receive what is on offer in the National Curriculum at times wish for their religious and cultural values to be respected and their moral position accommodated.[114] It is quite likely that many in the Pakistani community will wish for 'abstinence education' to be included in the sex and relationship curriculum.

RELIGION AND CULTURE

"Asian immigrants differ from the host population in important respects—language, religion, culture and social organisation"
Phillip Jones.

As I write this, the front page of my newspaper is talking about Justice Cook, who is a member of the Christian Lawyers' Fellowship and who jailed a woman for carrying out an illegal abortion. So, by discussing religion, I know I am entering controversial territory. But, we have been told by the government that we are heading towards Birmingham becoming a Muslim-majority city and that religion is important to Muslims, including those who may not 'practice' all its requirements. So, controversial it may be, I believe it is essential that we take a new look at the place of religion in our city.

Remember 1857!

It has been stated that, during their rule in India, the intentions of the British were to better the 'natives' of India. Early on, the British discovered that the cultural practices and religious beliefs of the people they had conquered in India had presented bigger barriers than anything else they had ever encountered.

It is now well known that religion was cause of the first war of independence in 1857. There may have been other grievances but this acted as a trigger. Apparently, the Indian soldiers were issued cartridges which had been greased with animal fat. This had offended both Hindu and Muslim sensibilities. This then started a rumour that the British outsiders had sought to destroy the religion of local people. It was after this war that the British Crown had taken over the affairs of the East India Company and had begun to directly rule the country from London. From this and much more besides, we should have known that for Asians their religion and culture is very important and they were not going to easily give it up and assimilate.

The ex-cricketer Pakistani politician Imran Khan was quoted asking: why can't the West understand? "When I first went to England, I was shocked to see the depiction of Christianity in Monty Python's 'Life of Brian.' This is their way. But for us Muslims, the Holy Koran and the Prophet, peace be upon him, are sacred. Why can't the West accept that we have different ways of looking at our religions?"

There is a story, from the 1960s, of a Pakistani bus driver. It was time for prayer so he stopped his bus to pray on the roadside. For the second generation religion is equally important, for some even more than their parents. Over 20 years ago, research told us that for nearly all Muslim second generation people they spoke to, their religion was 'important' or 'very important'. [115] Data gathered in schools in the Hodge Hill area has backed this. Two of the four wards had high numbers of Pakistanis—41.5% and 50.5%. The findings showed that Muslim students placed a high value on religion both as identity marker and as a moral compass. They were more likely to agree with the importance of tolerance, courtesy, justice, loyalty, trust and honesty; more positive than other ethnic groups about trusting people in their own community and most positive about citizenship as a subject. Pakistani students displayed far more trust of their teachers than the other groups. [116]

In the mid 1980s, Daniele Joly had shown the Pakistani parents commitment to the religious education of their children. [117] The early findings of my doctoral research amongst local Pakistani parents in 2013 would lead me to conclude that they are as committed as they were then to their children learning the Quran, Islamic Studies and Urdu.

The sociologist Peter Beger wrote in New York Times in 1968: "(By) the twenty-first century, religious believers are likely to be found only in small sects, huddled together to resist a worldwide secular culture." This could have been said about Birmingham at the time. The trouble is we have all gone on thinking that Berger's prediction had become reality when in Birmingham the opposite has been happening with the arrival, first of Black Christians and then large numbers of Muslims. A number of other migrant groups have also added to the 'religious' group in our city.

Doing more of what we did in the past will not be sufficient. The situation facing us will require new thinking. The future facing our city community has not been lived by anyone so we do not have the luxury of learning from their experience. Therefore, following in the tradition of the Lunar Men, we have to use our best understanding and insight to face it; even shape it. Professor Michael Clarke, Birmingham University has said, in his introduction to the 'Good City' report[118] that our city was "becoming a new kind of European city for which we have no precedents, and it poses hard questions for those who lead it now or who wish to lead it in the future." This is truer in relation to religion than anything else.

According to Jurgen Habermas we are currently witnessing a transition from a secular to a "post-secular society" in which "secular citizens" have to express a previously denied respect for "religious citizens." While church attendance seems to have gone down (with some exceptions from the independent churches) attendance at mosques does not seem to be declining. This presents a challenge to many who work in our public services. They had thought that religion had been put to bed for good, well out of sight. Maybe it had but it is waking up and increasingly demands recognition. I remember being told by a school in Northfield that 36% of its parents had said they had no religion. This seemed very different from the kind of response one would find in Sparkhill or Saltley. Sadly, much of the discussion on minorities in the city has centred on 'race' and hardly any attention has been paid to religion and culture which are, sometimes more integral for Pakistani-Birmingham

It is official: "There is religious discrimination against Muslims"

One of the best reference publications on this is the report 'Islamophobia' from the Runnymede Trust. It was published in 2004. It resulted from the work of a diverse group of experts from across the faith communities. Included in its membership were Dr Phillip Lewis and Reverend John Webber, interfaith advisers for the Bishop of Bradford and Bishop of Stepney respectively. Of course, long before the publication of this national report, the Muslim community knew about Islamophobia as it was on the receiving end of what was described by Peter Latchford as a 'social evil'. In Birmingham, the earliest official reporting of this Muslim-directed racism, was in the Birmingham Pakistan Forum report

'Pakistanis in the 1990s and Beyond' which had been published, jointly with Birmingham City Council, in 1996. It was described as 'Islam phobia' (page 107)

In her contribution to the above 'Good City' report, Dr Jagbir Jhutti-Johal[119] said: "the good city is a city that meets the needs of all its citizens. Employment opportunities, education and public services must be accessible to all." We need to make sure this applies to Pakistanis and Muslims.

Muslims who were interviewed for DWP 360 report pointed to a catalogue of issues which included: "being refused employment because of a dress code, stereotyping, low representation, discrimination for wearing traditional or religious dress to interviews, prayer facilities, and religious holidays." They also identified some of these issues as limits on their career progress. Given below are a few of the extracts from the above report:

- Employers preferring to recruit people from their own ethnic background on the basis of uncertainty and fear of the unknown. Non-White Muslims suffering double discrimination: for being from an ethnic minority group and for being Islamic . . . . 'pure Islamic penalty':
- Islamophobia has exacerbated prejudice and discrimination, making it harder at present for Muslims than most other groups to get a fair chance in the labour market.
- Experts pointed to different kinds of racisms, one of which was anti-Asian racism which impacted most particularly on working-class Asians, most of whom are Pakistani and Bangladeshi. They also pointed out that the cultural racism had shifted into racism against Muslims
- Even though they could not prove, people had strong perceptions of discrimination. Most Muslims believed employers would discriminate against them because of their ethnicity, and increasingly because of their religion. People believed that their Asian names counted against them.
- Wearing of non English clothes a turn off for employers, especially ones that identify people as Muslims. People cited men having beards and women wearing scarves as the possible reason for their lack of success at interviews.

- Employers having concerns about employing Muslims because they could not accommodate their religious needs, but also because they were concerned they would not fit in with other workers. Employers could (refuse jobs to Muslims) employ other Asians and still fulfill their equal opportunities recruitment criteria.

According to the above report, approximately half of the discrimination was due to people's ethnicity, the other half was to do with their being a Muslim. It has been referred to as 'double penalty'. Elsewhere, it has been pointed out that Pakistanis were disadvantaged by their poorer characteristics such as lower levels of English language fluency and human capital in general. So, does that make it a 'triple penalty'—social class, ethnicity and religion? What about for Pakistani women? Is there a fourth dimension to disadvantage for them? The report has suggested that "cultural and religious awareness training amongst employers could help address this." For us, this would mean a *city-wide programme on religion but with a particular focus on Islam and Muslims.* As well as employers, I would include service providers gaining such awareness. Could we also include the general population in such an endeavour so to enable people to gain an understanding of each others' beliefs and values?

RELIGION
BIRMINGHAM PUPILS 2011

	Primary	Secondary	Special	All
	%	%	%	%
Buddhist	0.2	0.2	0.2	0.2
Christian	20.0	26.1	26.8	22.6
Christian RC	9.5	11.4	7.5	10.2
Hindu	1.3	1.7	0.7	1.5
Jewish	0.1	0.1	0.0	0.1
Muslim	37.5	34.3	29.7	36.0
Sikh	2.4	3.9	1.4	3.0
Other	1.2	1.9	3.3	1.5
No Religion	12.7	12.2	18.6	12.6
Not Known	15.2	8.1	11.7	12.2
Total	100	100	100	100

Based on compulsory school age pupils excludes PRU data

'There is always Ladypool Road'!—eating out for Pakistanis

In his now famous 'sleepwalking to segregation' speech, Trevor Phillips, the then Head of the Equality and Human Rights Commission had outlined the features of an integrated society to include equality: of treatment and fair outcomes: participation: decision-making and responsibility for society's success and interaction: "no-one should be trapped within their own community, and in the truly integrated society; who people work with, or the friendships they make, should not be constrained by race or ethnicity."[120] In my view, our alcohol culture and lack of halal food in many restaurants act as constraints for integration. In his speech he had said that in our most distinguished universities, you can pick out the invisible 'no Blacks need apply' messages. I believe there are 'No Pakistanis wanted here' signs in many places across the city. These maybe invisible to some but are visible enough to those they are aimed at. Some are even disguised as 'welcome' signs.

The city's nighttime economy is well known. Large parts of the city centre and a number of local shopping and social centres come alive during the evenings and weekends. The significance of this economy was marked during last September when, for a whole week, the Council House was lit up in purple. Central to this economy is the role of alcohol and eating out. Yet, the activity involves few Muslim-background Brummies, who, following their religious and cultural socialisation, often do not drink.

Then there is eating-out. There are many hundreds of restaurants in the city, open most nights and who provide their customers with an opportunity to socialise. As well as being with one's own social network, during these occasions one is able to see strangers doing the same at nearby tables.

Avtar Johal has talked about how, in the 1950s, they used to march to pubs and clubs in order to put pressure on them to let Black and Asians in. This was with the help of university students. Of course, we don't now have restaurants refusing to serve ethnic minorities, do we?

An article in the New Statesman has drawn attention to this problem. Its author, Mehdi Hasan, pointed out that "most of the up market restaurants in London do not cater for the city's burgeoning Muslim population"[121]. I wondered what the situation was in my city. Do our top restaurants provide halal food? I know they do down in the Balti Triangle and down the Alum Rock Road but do they in the city centre restaurants, in the Mail Box, Brindley Place and the Jewellery Quarter. So, off I went with my research. The Advanced Research Methods module on my PhD course came in handy.

I searched 'top restaurants Birmingham'; we have so many. I then phoned them to ask the simple question, in the best and politest voice I could manage: "hello sir/madam. We would like to come and eat at your restaurant. I was wondering whether you served halal food." I phoned 5 or 6 restaurants. Not a single one said "yes sir, we do serve halal food and we would love to have you." I found the phoning hard work. I had to repeat everything, especially almost spell-out: halal. One even asked: "what is hal-hal?" It was as if I was speaking a foreign language and making unreasonable demands. Finally, when I was confronted by the manager of a posh restaurant, I gave up phoning. I didn't want to phone any more places. Actually I wanted to go round his establishment and remind him that he depended on customers like me. Or maybe he didn't. He gave me a very clear message in his "no we don't"; it put me in my place. He wasn't just cold; he was icy. He was saying: "you want halal; go down to your own restaurants!"

So, my conclusion was that this was not just a London issue. Of course, all the restaurants I did not phone may serve halal food. Here, in the place I call home, Muslims are told very clearly where to take their custom. They have to do without the Italian, Chinese or modern English cuisine in many of our city restaurants and eat yet another meal down at their local balti.

I can see good reasons for taking action on this matter. As well as it stopping such overt discrimination against a large section of our community, I am sure there is a business case that can be made. Surely, restaurants would like to attract more customers. It is not just a matter of going out in the evenings. Imagine, a Muslim is out shopping in the city centre during the day and they fancy something to eat other than the usual fish; what are they going to do; starve until they get home! I also believe that our restaurant industry is well capable of accommodating this need just as they responded to the demand for more vegetarian food.

In 1954, Henry Gunter had asked for a citywide campaign against problems facing ethnic minorities, I believe a similar coordinated effort across Birmingham has to be made to address the exclusion of Pakistanis and Muslims from the city restaurants. I also believe that our restaurant industry is well capable of accommodating this need just as they responded to the demand for more vegetarian food.

The Cantle Report had said that people lived separate lives—in education, community and voluntary bodies, where they worked, where they worshiped, language they spoke, their social and cultural networks. "These lives often do not seem to touch at any point, let alone overlap and promote any meaningful interchanges."[122] There are clear social benefits of eating together or at least in the same restaurants. It will surely help to bring together the parallel worlds that are Muslim-Birmingham and the rest-of-Birmingham. Imagine going out with your friends and family. The couple or group at the next table are Muslims sharing a meal. For once, they are not there as waiters but actually being served by someone. You may not talk to them but at least you are in the same place, doing the same thing as fellow humans.

Then there are benefits for work teams of having halal food in mainstream restaurants. Next time you plan a trip out for your multi-racial, multi-religious team, you will not be restricted to the same old balti restaurants.

Review of the alcohol culture

> "Well drink's everywhere, it doesn't matter where you go, even when you go to snooker halls and that you've got people drinking in there, so it's virtually every-where. Wherever you go there'll be drinking, drinking will be associated everywhere you go so you just take . . . keep myself to myself [Edit]. Generally amongst Muslims to see drink is hurtful you know" (Harun Rana, aged 25-34).

In my first job in the public sector, I worked as a youth worker. Our evening sessions used to finish at 10pm. This was a formal finishing time but invariably it took time to clear the centre of the young people. If they were in the middle of a pool game or some other activity, we showed some flexibility and waited until they had finished.

In those days, the closing time at pubs used to be 10.30pm. There was a pub just over the road from the centre. The practice was to send someone over before closing time so they could buy a round of drinks for everyone. I knew these gatherings were important. Later, I came to understand it as 'team-building'. We would talk about the work we had done, problems and issues, which kid is presenting a challenge, who is making progress, what was coming the next day, any long-term plans etc. As a junior member of the team, I certainly didn't want to miss out on all this. So I went along, made my half-pint last as long as I could, listen to what was being said, join in the conversation whenever I could and leave at the end or make my excuses and leave earlier.

A few years later, after qualifying as a teacher, I moved to work at a Community College in the Black Country. Our team of three had a tradition of going to a local pub for our lunch on Fridays. Then, after leaving my college job, I ended up back in Birmingham Education Department in 2001. During the ten years in the job, alcohol featured in much of our work socials and 'team building' sessions.

A recent article has acknowledged the role alcohol plays as a popular leisure activity in many contemporary societies and how it generates or fosters 'sociality and 'community'. The authors set to explore Muslim attitude to alcohol consumption and contribute to the debate about use of public space and cohesion. They conclude that, for Muslims, alcohol "is producing new unanticipated forms of exclusion . . . For those Muslims who do not drink, alcohol has the reverse impact on structures of feeling, generating emotions of disgust and repulsion." [123] Even, where non-alcoholic drinks are available, Muslims may choose not to enter these spaces because they are uncomfortable and feel 'out of place.

From a cohesion perspective, it has been pointed out that, in reaction to such alcohol-based culture, Pakistani Muslim young people end up creating their own "oppositional leisure spaces, such as small independent businesses, cafes, canteens and other types of social spaces . . . which help them to maintain their own faith value systems and strengthen their own religious commitments and identity . . ." These spaces can be commonly located in specific neighbourhood communities rather than the city centre and are not frequented by White-majority customers. A Headteacher of a local school with deep and longstanding knowledge of the Pakistani community told me that there are many young Pakistanis with potential to play top level football and other sports. Sadly, most stay away from sports clubs and teams given most have an alcohol culture.

Trevor Phillips spoke of Asian communities self-segregating from the mainstream. It is very easy to see this as 'choice' when in reality it is a product of the wider exclusionary forces due to the presence of alcohol and absence of halal food. In my view this constrains integration. Our restaurants and bars act as 'non-Muslim spaces'. Elsewhere, attention has been drawn to the excluding nature of urban regeneration. It has been pointed out that strategies to re-vitalise the night-time economies that are predicated on alcohol are implicitly excluding faith communities, such as Muslims and thus are potentially contributing to social segregation.

> *"You get a few comments at work when people say, I think when we used to finish at work for say the holidays like Christmas and so on and people used to say oh are you coming down the pub and so on after work, and I'd say 'oh no I don't drink'. [Then mimics his colleagues' response] 'What, you don't drink, have you got a life?' So obviously that shows what they think of drinking. Anyway, I say 'yeah, fine thanks, yeah I have a good life' actually but I don't drink, simple as that"* (Bazid Nazar, aged 25-34). [124]

The National Union of Students has published a report into women students' experiences of 'lad culture' in higher education[125]. Such an alcohol-dominated environment is said to present particular challenges for men and women from minority backgrounds, especially Muslims.

In cataloguing the above, I don't mean to give an impression that I am opposed to people drinking alcohol. I am merely drawing attention to the part alcohol plays in our society including the modern workplace. Maybe, it is time, in a city such as ours where so many current and future workers object to alcohol on religious and cultural grounds, for us to review our 'normal' practices. I would have thought it is not beyond us to come up with other ways to meet, to build our teams and generally have a good time as colleagues. As they say, there is more than one way to skin a cat.

Religion and education

I have been exploring the role of religion, with a particular reference to education. I list below some of the articles which point to new ways of looking at our situation:

- Should schools reinforce children's religious identity?—Mark Halstead
- Imams, ulema and Sufis: providers of bridging social capital for British Pakistani—Philip Lewis (Adviser to the Bishop of Bradford)
- Educational leadership: an Islamic perspective—Saeeda Shah
- Islamic values: a distinctive framework for moral education?—Mark Halstead

- Education and Islam: a new strategic approach—Maurice Irfan Coles
- Mosque improves pupils' attendance—Lucy Ward, The Guardian
- Union calls for end to single-faith schools—Polly Curtis, The Guardian (the article went onto say: "You could have imams coming in, you could have the rabbi coming in and the local Roman Catholic priest").

The articles provide food for thought. There are similar questions which can be asked, no doubt, for other service areas. For example, what about faith healing in relation to health? Some may think it irrational and unscientific. But, many in our city believe it works. Each week in my Urdu newspaper, there are adverts for Faith Healers. At our local Farmers' Market, each month there is a group called 'Healing on the Streets.'

I did a recent consultancy for a Birmingham school which serves a mainly Muslim community. Following are some extracts from the report which was produced for them:

- Negative attention paid to religion especially Islam
- Little exploration within education of the positive potential of religious belief.
- I was told "faith has much more presence" at the school compared to other schools and that "discipline is different because of culture and faith."
- School and mosques finding between them ways of serving the needs of young people in better ways. The need to find, in partnership with parents and religious leaders, creative ways to reduce mosque attendance by the young people by delivering instead some of the teaching within the school environment. Also, setting properly equipped and resourced homework groups at the mosque schools
- Greater liaison between schools and mosques. I was told: "for something that impacts on so many of our children's lives, it is surprising how little we know about mosque schools."

Then there is the importance of creating greater coherence in the lives of Pakistani young people with reference to the messages they receive from home, mosque and school. We know from research on the 'Catholic effect' that this can have a better outcome for young people and the wider community. This has pointed out that a learning environment culturally (or religiously) consonant with the parents' is more likely to produce healthy learning outcomes for young children and is more likely to foster a firmer sense of self.

Modood has pointed to two biases which are relevant to Pakistani-Birmingham. One was to see the position of visible minorities where the "focus was on issues such as colour-racism, poverty, educational underachievement, drugs, crime, and children brought up by single mothers." The second was a secularist bias which failed to recognise the role of religion and religion-based culture. We know that for a long time this has been central to the Pakistani community. The author also stated that "in Britain virtually nobody, policy makers, the media or academics, talked about Muslims until the late 1980s, the time of the Salman Rushdie affair."[126]

After-school religious classes

Research nationally and locally has shown that most Pakistani young people spend a significant amount of time, especially in their early years, at a mosque or Islamic centre. The City Council has done some work on this matter already but more is needed.

In 2012, I was asked to use my skills in Urdu and English language to help with the facilitation of a seminar in a West Midlands Local Authority[127]. It had been organised by their interfaith network. The delegates from the local Pakistani community pointed out that religion was very important to them. They wanted their children to have a proper understanding of Islam and to be able to read the Quran. They also valued their children to be taught Urdu so they could communicate with the older generation and appreciate their cultural heritage.

They considered it important that religious teachers were properly qualified and able to provide authentic education. However, the community was very keen for Urdu to be taught in mainstream, schools.

Delegates pointed out that work in religious schools can be very challenging given poor resourcing. "There can be a hundred children with just one teacher. Some of the children can have learning disabilities and behaviour challenges." They also drew attention to their exclusion from the policy process. "Services are often designed somewhere else and imposed on minorities. Minority perspectives are often an after-thought. It should be central to such design."

Following the event, I pointed out that much of what had been raised at this event would probably also apply to Birmingham; these were not matters exclusive to their community. Perhaps, a regional approach should be taken across the West Midlands.

A Pakistani officer, from their Safeguarding Children Board said that there was a need for local authorities to acknowledge more fully the needs of children who need an Islamic education and specific language teaching.

Muslim delegates recommended greater investment in the religious institutions and for accredited training to be provided to help equip the mosque teachers.

Religious Education in schools; more not less!

For many years, our schools across the country have had RE on the curriculum. This has meant that wherever one was educated one would learn about different religions which are now an integral part of our society. Since 1988 local authorities have had a duty to establish a Standing Advisory Council for Religious Education (SACRE). These bodies are made up of representatives of different faiths. They agree the syllabus for their local schools. I am told that these bodies are now being disregarded by the new Academies which are outside of Local Authority control. According to the recent figures there are over 2000 such schools. There are a growing number of such academies in Birmingham. I hope they will continue to stay within the SACRE framework. Shifting their accountability away from the local authority to central government is one thing; they need to remember that they are still educating future citizens of this city community.

RE is also being downgraded in other ways. According to the Times Educational Supplement, less is being spent on the subject per pupil. There has been a reduction of specially trained RE teachers and less time is allocated to the subject on the timetable.

While nationally RE is slowly being removed as an important subject, here in Birmingham we need it more than ever. The subject for me plays a central role in the development of a multicultural community. All of the arguments for its inclusion in the school curriculum which were presented in the Swann Report still hold true, regardless of the colour of the national politics or the prejudices and biases of politicians responsible for our schools. Under a heading 'The Case for Religious Education', it presented three reasons why religious education is considered to be a crucial element in the education process. [128]

Firstly, it is argued that in order for a young person to be considered fully educated, they must have some understanding of the nature of belief and of different belief systems and of how these have and are still influencing human experience. Such knowledge can, by extension, help in the formation of pupils' own personal beliefs and values, whether religious or non-religious. It quoted from the Durham Report:

> '. . . *Religious education has a place in the educational scene on educational grounds. where education is understood as the enriching of a pupil's experience, the opening up of a pupil to all the influences which have coloured his or her environment . . . The existence of a religious interpretation of life is a fact of history and of present human experience. There are many millions of men and women throughout the world who find through their religious beliefs a deep meaning and purpose for their lives and a system of values by which their lives can be lived. There appears to be a "spiritual dimension" in man's nature which requires to be expressed by "religion" of one kind or another.*
>
> *By religion we mean some pattern of belief and behaviour related to the questions of man's ultimate concern.*
>
> *Man seems to have to find "a faith to live by"; however noble. or simple, or debased. Young people share in the human condition. They should have some opportunity to learn that religion is a feature of this condition. and for some men a deeply significant area of human knowledge and experience.'* [129]

Secondly, it is argued that an understanding and appreciation of religious diversity contributes to, and is indeed vital to, the development of a young person's understanding of the motivations, values and outlook of people from a range of religious backgrounds, both within this society and in other societies—as the Berkshire agreed syllabus for religious education puts it:

> *'Religious education contributes to international understanding in the world as a whole, and to community relations within Britain.*

> *Increasingly we live in one world, and increasingly Britain is a multicultural, multi-faith society. It is vital that citizens should be familiar with a variety of beliefs and customs, and that they should have insight into the underlying values and concerns which different cultures and societies have in common.'*

Thirdly, it is argued that religious education provides a basis and a context for a school's programme of moral education.

> *'. . . the insights and accumulated wisdom of the great world religions cannot be ignored in any comprehensive scheme of moral education.'*

The 'moral' dimension of religious education also relates directly to some of the fundamental concerns raised by the multi-racial nature of our society, most notably perhaps the need to tackle racism and injustice and to seek to create true equality of opportunity for youngsters from all ethnic groups, which we would see as central to 'Education for All'. As the Berkshire agreed syllabus again explains:

> *'Religious education . . . develops consideration for other people, respect for moral and legal obligations, and concern for fairness and justice in society at large.'*

For many of our children RE has provided one of the few opportunities to learn about the beliefs and values of their city neighbours. Even those people who vandalised Bournville College thinking it was a mosque will have had some exposure to beliefs of their Muslim neighbours. Before the subject is done away with, we would be well advised to listen to the experts.

According to the European Commission Project on Religion, Education, Dialogue and Conflict, irrespective of their religious positions a majority of students are interested in learning about religions in school. They pointed out that the main preconditions for peaceful coexistence between people of different religions are "knowledge about each other's religions and worldviews, shared interests, and joint activities." It was found that those "who learn about religious diversity in school are more willing to enter into conversations about religions and worldviews with students from other backgrounds than those who do not have this opportunity for learning." The experts, drawn from across Europe, have advised that stereotypical images of religions should be countered and, instead, a more complex picture should be presented of the impact of religion on society and the individual. They have also pointed out the importance of having 'competent' teachers, both through initial training and continuing professional development.[130]

Religion as a 'good'

I agree with Tariq Modood who has said, on more than one occasion, that religion should no longer be seen as something private. It should be allowed to come out into the public square and its followers should be allowed to see the world around them from their religious eyes. This is very necessary in Birmingham with implications for areas such as health, education, employment, law and order to name a few. There has been some recent recognition of the potential good of religion. I believe we need to build on this. We know, for example, that religion can have a positive influence in raising educational standards but this has not been explored with reference to Islam. Research into the lives of Black Christian young people has shown that their religious beliefs and the religious communities they were a part of were considered to have a significant impact on their academic success. Some researchers have spoken of 'religion as social capital' which provides a strong impetus for young people to pursue education and achieve high standards. I plan to explore this area further with reference to my PhD research on Pakistani boys in Birmingham.

A number of studies have documented the benefits of religious involvement. It has been shown that religious people tend to be healthier, live longer and have higher levels of subjective well-being. At the societal level, higher religious involvement is related to lower crime rates, increases in civic involvement, higher levels of cooperation, lower divorce rates, higher marital satisfaction and better child adjustment.

There is evidence which points to religion providing not only a barrier to negative masculine peer culture but also as a positive influence. Generally, there might be a moral panic about Pakistani and Muslim young people, but locally things have not been too bad. For example, few of them were involved in the 2011 Birmingham riots as pointed out by Peter Latchford OBE in his report. It showed that Asians, at 19%, were the smallest group involved. He put it down to "Muslim families having a better handle on their youth."[131]

It is important to recognise that the city was a pioneer in how it responded to the arrival of Muslims. But, then it has been a pioneer in many other ways too before its policies and some practices began to take a backward direction. In 1988 the Education Department issued a Guidance document[132] to help schools to make an effective response to Muslim pupils.

The Swann Report had said:

> "We firmly believe that if the message of this report is accepted by schools and the changes in perspective and emphasis which we have advocated—particularly in relation to religious education, 'pastoral' concerns and language needs—are realised, then this will go a considerable way towards meeting the concerns of many ethnic minority parents about their children's education and that many of the particular concerns which have led sections of the Asian community to call for the establishment of their own schools would also be allayed . . . ." (page 509)

Dr Chris Hewer, the then Interfaith Adviser for the Bishop of Birmingham, had posed a similar challenge to the education system:

> "Can the state embrace the opportunity of using a religious ethos and an Islamic perspective as part of its strategy to raise the educational standards of children from disadvantaged minority communities?"[133]

Some employers, services and neighbours may not have been exposed to Pakistani needs, because they lived 'somewhere else'. There was a time not very long ago when the Pakistani community was mainly to be found in inner city wards. As discussed earlier, this has changed. Increasingly, Pakistanis and Muslims are no longer 'somewhere else' but increasingly to be found across the city. This presence will, no doubt, increase as will the need for employers and service providers to be more 'Pak-friendly' in their work.

Some schools in the city have done a great deal to accommodate and show respect for the religious needs of their staff and students. The Christian chair of governors of a mainly Muslim school once told me of their efforts in "sensitive catering for the needs of Muslim pupils (facility for Friday prayers enabled by a small time table change, shortened breaks during Ramadan, halal food etc) and also . . . the appointment of an increasing proportion, about 30% of Asian and Muslim staff . . . ." However, it has been pointed out to me that, when it comes to connecting with their Pakistani students' wider lives, many schools tend to do so only when things go wrong and few rarely connect with their religious lives. Another school is also a leader in how it has responded to the the religious needs of Pakistani young people. They have also made changes to their timetable to accommodate lunchtime prayers. I have been told that on Fridays, they have some 500 student praying in the school hall.

One head teacher I know, a practising Christian, has developed relationships with local Muslim leaders as soon as he arrived at his school. On a number of occasions, he has addressed gatherings at local mosques. A newly-retired head teacher said to me that a Muslim expert in religion and education had once commented to her: "if all the schools were like yours in how you accommodate the needs of the Muslim community, there would be no need for Muslim schools."

The opposite is sadly also true. One school I know is struggling in this respect. Located in the very leafy suburbs, its leadership told me that it has seen a rise in numbers of Muslim pupils. A number of the students have requested space for prayer. The school's head teacher said to me: "we don't know what to do. We have seen ourselves as a secular school, not a religious one. We have never had such requests before." The conversation for me summed up the current situation in Birmingham in terms of multicultural issues.

While the City Council support infrastructure has been removed as a consequence of the cuts in funding, the need for it has increased. There appears to be a shortage of "authoritative and trusted" advice. The above school also pointed out to me that many of the White parents are worried that "we are becoming a Muslim school" (about a third of the school pupils are Muslim which for some of the parents are too many especially when they see "all the headscarves"). It would seem that the situations like this are nothing new where population movement has resulted in school staff "confronting a new situation where they have no prior knowledge of the way of life of their Muslim pupils."[134] In this developing situation, I would contend that, more than before, there is a role for our local SACRE. Our schools could do with being issued updated guidance to help them properly accommodate the cultural and religious needs of their Pakistani pupils.

In a recent article, the Times Educational Supplement said that "textbooks must turn the page with Islam." This is nowhere as important as it is in Birmingham where Muslims are now the largest religious group in our schools.

We as a city have done some exemplary work on *madrassah*, religious, schools where many of our Muslim pupils spend their time after school. An excellent DVD was produced 'We are all citizens'. All schools and organisations working with young people should be provided a copy and encouraged to use the resource. This would help to challenge some of the misunderstandings and stereotypes people have about Muslims.

From time to time I go into schools to raise staff and students' awareness of diversity. I pose questions such as: who was Al-Ghazali; what alcohol, alkali and algebra have in common or, at a more general level, the Islamic contribution to civilisation. Not surprisingly, I find the understanding level of teachers to be quite poor in this respect. This is not their fault but of the system that has educated them and whose priorities for their continuing professional development do not include these matters. Teachers and others could turn to the US President Barack Obama for the answers. On 4 June, 2009, he said the following at Cairo University:

> *"As a student of history, I also know civilisation's debt to Islam. It was Islam—at places like Al Azhar—that carried the light of learning through so many centuries, paving the way for Europe's Renaissance and Enlightenment. It was innovation in Muslim communities that developed the order of algebra; our magnetic compass and tools of navigation; our mastery of pens and printing; our understanding of how disease spreads and how it can be healed. Islamic culture has given us majestic arches and soaring spires; timeless poetry and cherished music; elegant calligraphy and places of peaceful contemplation. And throughout history, Islam has demonstrated through words and deeds the possibilities of religious tolerance and racial equality."*

The Times Educational Supplement (20.09.2011) ran an article entitled: 'The teachers with a tabloid grasp of Islam'. It was subtitled 'All bombs and burqas'. Its opening paragraph made clear what teachers think about the religion:

> *Terrorism is an intrinsic part of Islam, all religious Muslim women wear the hijab, and the image that best represents the religion is a bomb.*

According to the article, the researcher Lynn Russell, Canterbury Christ Church University, found that teachers' understanding of Islam was largely formed by the media. The majority also believed that arranged marriages were required by Muslim law. A quarter said that they would struggle to teach about women in Islam because of their personal feelings on the matter.

Rosemary Rivett, of the National Association of Teachers of Religious Education, was not surprised by the findings. She thought outdated text books were to blame. Then again, "I could look at some of the books about Christianity and find the same thing."

This reminded me of a conversation with my son in the first couple of years of his primary school. I must have asked him what he was going to be when he grew up. He said to me, "I cannot be a scientist because I am brown and all the scientists are always White." I was shocked. Later that day, we sat in front of the computer and learnt about all the Chinese, Indian and Arab scientists. I then wrote a letter to his Headteacher in the hope they will provide a different education for their pupils.

I remember this quote from CLR James, from his foreword to 'the Black Jacobins':

> *I was tired of reading and hearing about Africans being persecuted and oppressed in Africa, in the Middle Passage, in the USA and all over the Caribbean. I made up my mind that I would write a book in which Africans . . . . would themselves be taking action*

I then had an 'imaginary' dream about a different future. I dreamt seeing a reply to the above article on religious ignorance which had been written by an officer of the City Council, with responsibility for religious and cultural understanding:

Dear Editor

In response to your article on teachers' lack of knowledge about Islam (Teachers with a tabloid knowledge of Islam 20.9.11), I am writing to let you know that things are very different in Birmingham. Our statistics last year showed that Muslims are the largest religious group in our schools. They currently make up 36%, with all the Christian denominations put together coming to 34%.

We have solid foundations in this respect. During the 1960s, we were the local authority others, including the government of the day, were turning to for advice on immigrant education. Later, we were also pioneers in publishing guidance on education of Muslim children. This was a 40 page document, one half in English and the other half Urdu, which had been produced by our Muslim Liaison Committee. It had a Foreword written by the then Chief Education Officer Professor Sir Tim Brighouse. At the time this was published we were also seen as a site for good practice on anti-racist multi-cultural education.

With reference to teaching in Birmingham, you will note from our website the following "Commitment to equality of opportunity":

> *A strong commitment to equality of opportunity at all levels throughout the service and commitment to taking positive action to increase members from groups currently under represented in the teaching profession.*
>
> *To strengthen our multi-cultural, anti-racist and Equal Opportunity perspective we have three major aims:*
>
> *To be aware of and to counter racism and discriminatory practices;*
>
> *To be aware of and to provide for the particular needs of pupils with regard to their ethnic, cultural, historical, linguistic and religious backgrounds;*
>
> *To prepare all pupils for life in our multi-cultural society and build on strengths of cultural diversity."* [135]

We see relationships being central to the teaching and learning process. It helps when teachers have a proper understanding of the pupils and their background. We also have a belief in the value of the learning that takes place during the 85% of students' lives that they spend away from the classroom. So, for us, the education of our young people is a partnership between the teachers who work in our schools and their communities. And, we recognise that for such partnerships to work, our teachers need to understand their communities and their heritage.

To make the above a reality, we now have a programme of professional development for all teachers to equip them with knowledge of cultural and religious diversity, with all its complexities. All our new recruits, whatever job they do in our schools and at whatever level, are expected to come with a deep understanding of our community and its background. And those who do not have such an understanding are appointed on the condition that they will acquire the knowledge within their first year. To this effect, we have a number of centres and libraries dotted around our large city which provide a range of resources on religions and the cultural backgrounds of our main communities. We are also working with teacher training colleges and universities so that their programmes of initial training cover the necessary subject matter as a central part of their courses. It is worth pointing out that we provide similar training support and resources on Christianity and a range of other faiths which are present in the city.

So, as you can see, the future of Birmingham, which, according to government predictions, is the first to become a Muslim city, is precious to us. We certainly cannot afford those who teach our future citizens to have tabloid knowledge of Islam or indeed any other religion. And, of course, in this city which became home to the Dissenters in the 1700s, we cannot forget the large section of our community who do not subscribe to any religion whatsoever or those whose cultural or ethnic affiliation is ambiguous.

So, next time you have an opportunity to publish a similar article in your esteemed journal, perhaps you would be good enough to take a look at our innovative practice. Our motto as always: we are different; we are Birmingham.

I then came into the reality where religion is seen as private and its teaching in our schools is being downgraded let alone employers and service providers giving it any importance.

Respect for religion

I once spotted a picture of Prince William and the Duchess of Cambridge waiting to go into a mosque. They were sitting there without their shoes and the Duchess had her head covered. What are the implications for service providers, with a secular approach, providing services in our city with an increasing religious population? Do organisations provide guidance on appropriate dress for employees who may, as a part of their job, be visiting places of worship such as a mosque? One of the mosque leaders at the West Midlands event I facilitated stated that secular staff of organisations at times can be disrespectful in such situations.

According to the Joseph Rowntree Foundation, "Religious and cultural identity was very important to many people from minority ethnic communities but it was rarely responded to by mainstream service providers." [136]

'Fasting and prayer don't concern the doctors . . . they don't even know what it is';

The first page of this article said it all. It began with these words: "Pakistani Muslims have the poorest overall health profile in Britain, for reasons which at present remain poorly understood." The article highlights the considerable impact of religious identity on decision-making for many Pakistani Muslims and on their communication with practitioners. [137]

Across the UK, Pakistanis feel they are unwelcome in many health services. This affects the psychosocial well-being of Pakistani Muslims and their ability to manage long-term conditions. Their religion plays a central role in many patients' lives and helps them to make sense of their illness. They do not discuss religious matters with health practitioners due to a lack of confidence in their knowledge of such matters. They were described as 'highly qualified yet ignorant'. "The education they have received has proved inadequate to the situation they are faced with. It is inexcusable because the population change has not happened overnight."

For the patients, religious teachings and prayer or reading the Qur'an helped them to cope better with illness and helped decrease anxiety and depression. They would often use religious expressions naturally within conversations about health: "Just leave it up to Allah. What else can you do? . . . you have to do that, otherwise there's no life."

Prayer and attendance at religious gatherings increased patients' emotional resilience and ability to cope with illness, helping individuals be more patient with their condition and, particularly pain or anxiety.

It would seem that on matters of religion and culture, Pakistani patients and health practitioners live in very different worlds. Findings indicate that Pakistani Muslims consider reference to faith an appropriate response to diagnosis of long-term illness. As they don't understand religious and cultural matters, the doctors think such things are not important.

Shared understanding of religious and cultural matters is essential to effective patient-practitioner partnership. Poor professional knowledge leads to inadequate support for patients and poor response to their health needs. Increased knowledge and confidence to effectively engage with Muslim patients would help practitioners avoid situations that prevent or delay accurate diagnosis and intervention. Training practitioners to understand the cultural context of Muslim patients could provide such knowledge and confidence.

It has been pointed out that religion cannot replace ethnicity (or social class, gender or other aspects of identity) as a way of understanding Pakistani communities; it can contribute to a more complete picture of their experience.

So to sum up, on this contentious but integral subject, we are told that 25% of the national population have indicated in the recent census that they have 'no religion' while the figure is 19.3% in Birmingham. We know from the previous census that majority of people indicating as such are likely to be White. For example, Washwood Heath had the fewest people indicating 'no religion' followed by Bordesley Green while the city wards with the most people indicating 'no religion' were Moseley and Kings Heath and Selly Oak, with Weoley close behind.

The local expert Dr Chris Allen at Birmingham University, tells us about the increased presence of religion in our society. He points out that regardless "of whether you 'do' or 'don't do god', faith cannot be overlooked or disregarded. Faith today inspires and influences and it can lead people to act in both positive and negative ways. Faith undeniably exists . . ."[138] This is particularly so given the increased presence of 'minorities' in our city, who according to the Home Office Citizenship Survey, are more religious than the White majority. This was based on 15000 interviews across England and Wales, of whom 74% had described themselves as Christian and 2% as Muslim. The research pointed out that faith affiliation meant different things for different groups. Followers of minority religions "tended to feel their beliefs were more fundamental to their sense of self-identity compared to many White Christians" (p vii). When asked to identify ten things that said something about them, Muslims, Hindus, Sikhs and Black Christians identified religion as second (after family), while for the rest of the Christians, it was the seventh.[139]

In talking about the role of religion in our society, Brian Gates at St Martin's College has used the analogy of a car: we notice its visible appearance and performance but not what is under its bonnet and yet the latter is its major determinant.[140] If for no other reason than the fact that the Pakistani community is more religious than most, it is time we took a closer look at religion, not just Islam, in order to understand what shapes our citizens' values.

THE LONGBRIDGE MOSQUE THAT WASN'T!

I know the area very well. A few years ago I had researched the work of schools and organisations in the area to understand how they were responding to the needs of the White working class young people.

My work involved getting 'under the skin' of one school: Colmers. It is so close to the old car factory at Longbridge that one of its previous head teachers used to say that at times it felt as if there was an underground tunnel between the school and the factory. Apparently, the young people used to see their future lives only in relation to a job at the factory and little else. It was during this research project that I had met the local MP Richard Burden.

During my work in the area I also learnt how insulated the community, especially the young were. One Headteacher had said that when their pupils talked about 'going uptown', they did not mean the city centre but the shops in Northfield. The community seemed to be a million miles away from Saltley and Sparkbrook. And yet, I felt the people had much in common with the inner city communities. Neither knew much about the other. It was very pertinent to see Pakistani Network use the word 'insulated' about their own community. I used to think it would be great to have schools in this edge of Birmingham twin with their inner city counterparts. When, in 2000, I had said in my submission to the Lawrence Commission that we should promote greater understanding between the Inner and the Outer Ring, by the latter I could have meant this area. We have much work still to do as illustrated by a little news item in the Times Educational Supplement. When I read about a mosque being vandalised in the area, I could contextualise the incident. It also provided a metaphor for a 'parallel lives'-Birmingham.

The little news item was tucked away in the back pages. When I looked again, I realised that this was the result of a rumour being spread by anti-Muslim elements in the locality. The 'mosque' was actually the new Bournville College of Further Education in Longbridge[141].

The College Principal was quoted as saying: "I have heard that there are people within the local community spreading the rumour around that this is in fact a mosque, categorically it never has been a mosque. It has gone through planning and planning clearly identifies it as a conference centre. It doesn't even look like a mosque so how people are jumping to this conclusion I don't really know." He confirmed a window had been broken in the centre.

When I first read about the vandalism incident, I wondered what the schools in the area had done or were doing in response. Was there an assembly about it? Did they perhaps address the issues in Citizenship lessons or anywhere else in the curriculum for that matter? Or, given that Community Cohesion is no longer a priority under the current government and it's education inspection body, Ofsted, schools were probably far too busy to worry about such matters.

In my contact with schools in Northfield, I have learnt about the recent arrival in their community of Somalis. In fact one head teacher went as far to say that their best and most motivated students were the new arrivals.

Of course, many of the Somalis are Muslims. When a building is vandalised in their neighbourhood because it was mistaken for a mosque, what does this say to them? Or indeed what does it say to the Muslims in Birmingham generally about the kind of people their fellow Brummies are. Maybe there are some Pakistanis or Muslims or Asians (the kind of people who would vandalise a college building thinking it was a mosque can't always tell the difference) who were considering leaving the inner city and relocate to the greener outskirts of the city. Now, they might reconsider their plans.

When I heard about the vandalism incident, I went to see for myself what the new building looked like. As I stood on the pavement near the college, a Muslim lady passed me. I wanted to ask her how it felt to live in the area. But, it seemed intrusive so I kept my question to myself.

When I mentioned the above incident to someone who lived in the area, he hadn't heard about the incident. However, he pointed out that something far worse had happened further up the Bristol Road. Apparently, sometime ago, a newly opened Muslim Centre had been burned down in Weoley Square and the British National Party had proudly used the photographs in their election literature. Anoop Nayak, based on his research in the Outer Ring, has spoken of the area being seen as 'White space', exclusive and excluding. It would appear that those who are seen to encroach that space are not welcome.

In 2001, Councillor Afzal, speaking at the Black Workers' Group Conference, had pointed out that anti-Muslim sentiment posed "a huge challenge to our city." He also pointed to the "worrying levels of ignorance that exists amongst our citizens about each other's faiths and ways of life." Have we done enough to counter this challenge? Incidents such as that surrounding the 'Longbridge Mosque' would indicate that much action is still needed before we can claim to have One Birmingham.

Birmingham's Pakistanis are on the move out from the inner city. However, those who might have been considering living in the foothills of the Lickeys, might think again after reading such stories. Some might consider it preferable to go on living their 'parallel life' in the safety of their own ethnic group and avoid the potential of what has been described as 'everyday racism'—in the street, on the bus, while shopping etc.

James Callaghan, the then Home Secretary had pointed out, in 1968, his party's commitment to the multicultural society. He had said that in such a society, there will be equality before the law and where all communities will have respect for each other; a society in which there will be unity in purpose and common allegiance. "But this ideal of a multi-racial society, to which all of us except the extremists are committed, will not happen of its own accord. It is something that has to be worked for. Our policies must establish the ends that we will." Elsewhere, he had said, "in matters of race, so much of our prejudice springs from ignorance and from fear. Knowledge and understanding are the essential prerequisites and are, therefore, the enemies of prejudice."

At an earlier time, during the debate on what came to be the Commonwealth Immigration Act 1962, Hugh Gaitskell had suggested the government should use "every educational means at their disposal to create tolerance and mutual understanding". In his now famous speech, in 1966, Roy Jenkins had spoken of equal opportunity being "accompanied by cultural diversity, in an atmosphere of mutual tolerance. He had also said that this was not something that will solve itself "without positive action".

One of the less known initiatives from Bill Clinton's presidency is the national dialogue he had instigated on race.[142] Dialogue had been defined as a forum that draws participants from as many parts of the community as possible to share personal stories and experiences, honestly express perspectives and develop solutions to community concerns. We need such dialogue in Birmingham.

Let's not forget the White Brummies!

In my submission to the Lawrence Commission in 2000, I had said that we need to include White people in any work on identity and equality. It has been pointed out that Whiteness has traditionally been the invisible centre of the 'race' equality debate. It is time we drew it into any debate on anti-racism[143]. I have restated my position in much of my work on educational underachievement amongst the White working class. The need to explore what it means to be White is more crucial in Birmingham than anywhere else, given that White young people have become a minority in many of our schools. It is not many years before Whites will be a minority overall.

Could we, perhaps, instigate a programme of 'White Studies' with the aim of exploring what it means to be White in multi-ethnic present-day Birmingham? We need to create opportunities so people in the majority ethnic group are able to explore what it means to be White without any connotations of racism. There is also a need for us all to understand uncomfortable concepts such as White privilege.[144] Anyone interested in exploring this concept would be well advised to refer to the work of Tim Wise.[145]

FUTURE OF URDU IN THE CITY

We are on our way to becoming a bilingual city. At least 40% of our pupils are bilingual. Elsewhere in the document I have pointed out that there are a large number of children in Birmingham schools who have identified their home language as Urdu. What does this mean? How much Urdu do they know? Can they read it? Do they speak it? Or do they speak variations of Urdu and regional dialects? More critically, how effective is the Urdu provision for the 43,000 Pakistani pupils?

I would like to suggest that as a city we undertake some research to find out answers to the above questions. For now, my anecdotal research tells me that:

- Urdu is being offered in a number of city schools who take advantage of the fact that many of their pupils have learnt the language at the Madrassah and are able, with little additional input, to add to their exam figures
- Many of the Urdu teachers brought their skills from Pakistan and have had little input or investment in this country. There are very few British born teachers of Urdu
- Many of the young Pakistani teachers are either unable to teach the subject or do not wish to do so given its negative image
- Schools are under pressure to only employ 'good' teachers and it would appear that without the necessary training, Urdu teachers are not always "up to scratch"

To sum up, I spoke to one Headteacher who has nearly 40% Pakistani pupils and who has worked in other schools with a much larger presence from the community. I said: "what is the state of Urdu in other city schools?" His response included "awful" and "Urdu has died." He then proceeded to say: "I don't see an answer." We certainly need an answer! Sadly, the case of Urdu is not helped by the Pakistani community itself, some of whom, both here and in Pakistan, tend to approach the subject with a colonial mentality and see the language as worth less.

While at the above school, I also spoke to a teacher of Modern Foreign Languages. She spoke German and French as well as English. I was in the school to speak some Urdu to her Year 7 pupils. The teacher said to me she had been trying to learn Urdu. She said she had begun with a view that this was definitely 'too foreign' a language. But she persevered and was eventually able to overcome the barrier and made a start. In her email to me, she had used the words 'salaam' and 'shukerya'. I told her, I really appreciated what she was doing. It showed her respect for me and my mother tongue. Now that she had found out how hard it was, as an adult, to learn another language, we agreed that next time she comes across a Pakistani parent with little or no English, she was less likely to think: 'why don't they learn English'. I also went away, wondering whether it would be better, if we treated Urdu as a Modern Foreign Language rather than as a lesser status Community Language and whether this would help to take away its deficit label in the eyes of pupils, teachers and parents!

In terms of research, we need to explore:

- The importance of bilingualism/Urdu for young people's education. All the research tells us that knowing more than one language is better for students—intellectually, socially and economically
- What is the real nature of need for learners across the ages—views of learners (young and old), parents, teachers, school leaders?
- Urdu writers; who they are, what are they producing, their role in working with young people in schools; could this be integrated into an arts/literature strategy for the city/region?
- How to go about teaching Urdu to non-Pakistani young people and teachers?
- Resources and publications—what is available and what is needed further?

The information gathered could be used to produce an Urdu strategy for the city. I have drawn on my limited understanding of the example of the Welsh language and the progress they have made since passing the

Welsh Language Act 1993. At this stage I would like to suggest that we learn from what they have done in Wales on this matter. I am certainly not suggesting that Urdu has full equality with English only that we recognise it as a modern language that is shown respect and used as a basis for shaping our future city community. Maybe we could explore developing Urdu as a second language in Birmingham.

Part of the strategy would need to be recruitment and training and ongoing development of Urdu teachers. With the large number of spouses coming into the city from Pakistan, some of them have the potential to be trained in this role. If necessary, we could make a case to the Home Office that this is a shortage subject. During my days as Education Adviser for Birmingham, the government had relaxed immigration restrictions to allow in teachers of mathematics. A similar approach could be taken to bring in Urdu expertise from Pakistan. Some of this could be 'visiting expertise' to help us build our Urdu capacity.

It is necessary to point out here that part of the problem for languages such as Urdu is their association with immigrants. They are seen as 'less-than' 'proper' 'modern' languages such as French. I have often said that much of my success in this country has depended on my English competency, though as I have pointed out (see box), there is more to me than this. Also, there are times I want to ask people around me: 'I have learnt your language; how good is your Urdu?' That is when I have begun to think of myself as equal citizen with an equally worthwhile language and heritage.

We as a society and city need to change how we view other languages especially ones from migrant communities.

My mother tongue and other languages

I learnt my first words from Beyji and others in my family

But, it was not considered a 'proper' language (it was to me!); it had no name.

I then went to school; we had one teacher for all five classes

We sat in the dust. Here I learnt Urdu; much of it was foreign to me

I then went to big school; we could sit on benches here. Now I learnt Arabic, Farsi, English as well as Urdu

I was then sent to Vilayat

Everyone here told me "language = English"; nothing else mattered, nothing else counted

So I learnt English and . . . nothing else! I became fluent, even more than some who were born here

Then many, many years, I re-discovered my mother tongue. It even had a name this time. It is called Mirpuri, some call it Pahari

I also worked on my Urdu. I began to appreciate words I had neglected for many years

My world is a richer place now; and bigger! [146]

Solomos and Back pointed out how in City Council meetings multilingual South Asian councillors were heckled and asked to give a translation in English of their speech and how such "very crude abuse obviously has an effect . . ." They sum up the environment thus: "In the theatre of politics this constitutes a racism that is whispered in committee meetings and heckled from the side lines."

> *"Councillor Mohammad Afzal who has an accent . . . Afzal got up started to read the petition out, there were many interruptions from the opposition. There was all kinds of abuse like 'speak English', 'you are in England now' . . . . he hadn't finished because there were too many interruptions . . . it was pure racism . . . no doubt about it. They weren't interested in the issue it was all about language and pronunciation; they weren't interested in what was being said."*

Elsewhere, they quote one of their interviewees, a Black left-winger, saying:

> *"There was one particular meeting where we were preparing the left-slate for the AGM. One of my colleagues (a South Asian Councillor) was being put forward for a committee chair and one of my left colleagues stood up and said 'speaking quite frankly' that (the Councillor's) command of English was not good enough. I was extremely angry then; there it was suggested that this Councillor was incompetent. These comments were downright racist; (the south Asian Councillor) speaks five languages. I wonder how many (the White Councillor) speaks."*

This debate about language is central to Edward Said's Orientalism. The West's perspective which is the central plank of his book may have been fine at the time but surely needs a review. At the time the West and the East were supposedly worlds apart (never the twain etc) but things have changed somewhat with the movement of peoples we have had especially since World War II. Many of the people of the East, the Orientals, are no longer somewhere else but are actually a part of our world in the West. They (or should I say we as I belong to that world, having been born in the Orient and now being very much a part of the West's fabric) cannot be talked about as foreign, other, outsiders, pariahs. They are here and are, slowly, becoming a part of us.

It was one thing treating languages such as Urdu as second class to English in the days of the British Raj or in the early days of migration, it cannot be sustained. We are now educating young people who are second and third generation equal British citizens. Yet, we still seem to be using educational philosophies from the 1960s. For example, the way we talk about students being 'EAL' (English as Additional Language) is very much the language of the first government policy, Circular 7/65, issued in 1965. Surely, the students are bilingual and bicultural who move in and out of different languages and cultures. Such competence should, in my view, be seen as an asset rather than as a deficit.

REPRESENTATION AND GOVERNANCE

"None of the major institutions of local government and politics seems well adapted to dealing with race . . . . Race relations in Birmingham has been half a political issue because only half the case has been put—the case of coloured immigrants has yet to see the light of day as a force in local politics"—Newton

It has been pointed out that the problem for communities such as the Pakistanis is their lack of representation. According to Newton, "interests which are not forcefully pressed tend to be neglected, overlooked, ignored or denied" by White politicians. He explained that this was not because of their wickedness but because "they are most likely to respond to pressures from their own social group, whose social situation and political demands they know and understand, or from other social groups which can make life difficult." In such a situation, the groups which have the most difficulty "articulating their demands find the most difficulty in getting elites to respond to their demands with sympathy or with the knowledge of first-hand experience." So, it would seem that a community like the Pakistanis that is not organised and does not complain much could lose out in such a situation with the end result that their 'half' of the 'issue' is still waiting to be articulated. This is especially the case with those dimensions of 'Pakistani-ness' which are more to do with religion and culture and less with race.

I agree with Iris Young when she says that different groups in society have different perspectives. If those perspectives are to be represented properly in service organisations, the job is best done by people who come from within those groups. That would require members of the Pakistani community being on governing bodies of schools, colleges, universities and hospitals. There is no reason for such bodies not to have Pakistanis in proportion to their presence in the city's population or in their client population whichever is the greater. So for schools and colleges across the authority, that would require 25% Pakistanis on their governing bodies.

Given the overall Pakistani population and those affected by crime, as victims or perpetrators, surely it is unsustainable that a body such as the Birmingham Safety Partnership has no Pakistani staff and no Pakistani on its governing or decision-making structures. Of course, this also raises the issue of mandate. Those who do get onto such bodies need to remember that they are there as *representatives* of the Pakistani community and not for their own gain.

Danielle Jolly talked about the very large rally which had been organised in opposition to the publication of the Satanic Verses by the writer Salman Rushdie. Apparently, many of the Muslim Councillors had stayed away from the Council Meeting which followed the rally and where the matter was to be discussed. One wonders the reason for such an absence. Had someone twisted their arm? Did they, perhaps, have a legitimate reason to stay away from a meeting that was of extreme importance to their electors?

Abbas has drawn attention to the additional pressure which is sometimes applied on Muslim politicians. He has cited as example a letter, denouncing the events of 9/11, which had been presented, by Downing Street, to a number of the key Muslim politicians.[147] What is the situation for Pakistani Elected Members on Birmingham City Council? One Pakistani councillor told me that speeches are written for them and that they are not allowed to speak to the press. Whatever the truth of the matter locally or nationally, it does raise some questions about the possible restrictions placed on these politicians over and above their non-Pakistani colleagues.

Solomos and Back talked about the culture in the council house as alienating and on occasions hostile for ethnic minority councillors. "It is striking when one enters Birmingham's municipal centre, the Council House, that until very recently it has been an exclusively White preserve. As one walks through the corridors of the building, pictures of political notables are displayed and they are overwhelmingly White and male. The municipal culture itself is invested with a whole set of cultural assumptions about the heritage of its politicians."

Newton spoke of the dominant role played by paid Council officials. According to his perspective, it is the officers who have the upper hand.

He said: "the question we should ask is not 'do officers dictate policy?' but rather 'to what extent do officers control or influence policy decisions and under what sort of circumstances is this control or influence greater or smaller?'" His 'dictatorship of the official' thesis arises out of the relationship between officers and members being "essentially that between the highly trained expert with long experience of local government work and the unpaid, part-time, amateur politician who holds public office only as long as the swing of the electoral pendulum permits." He presented a long list of games officers play to get their own way. He called them 'techniques'. These included: writing long reports, full of technicalities and statistics, that committee members cannot possibly find time to read; or reports which are so short that they contain inadequate information for committee members to make their own decisions or withholding information. Does this go on in our council and how does it impact on bilingual Pakistani councillors? It would be worthwhile to undertake some qualitative research in order to find out what it is like to be a Pakistani councillor and a Pakistani employee of Birmingham council.

Solomos and Back referred to the 'colonial behaviour' of MPs Dennis Howell and Roy Hattersley. They also shed light on the selection of the successor to the above MPs, Roger Godsif, described as Mr Howell's "hand-picked successor" and who had "fixed" his own votes(page 108). We learn from the authors how the Pakistani Councillors Muhammed Afzal and Najma Hafeez had tried to challenge Mr Godsif. Apparently this did not go down well with the Birmingham Labour Party. Both these Councillors, as a result, had lost their positions as chairpersons of key Council committees. But "as a compensating gesture a south Asian supporter of Roger Godsif replaced Afzal on the Group Officers Executive" (p 147). "In the aftermath of Muhammad Afzal's challenge . . . two organisations linked with him had their funding withdrawn and their practices scrutinised" (p 148).

Maybe, in future we will see greater integrity in the selection of prospective candidates, leading to a few more Pakistani MPs in the city. Nationally, we have had all-female shortlists for Parliament and there has been talk that the Labour Party should have all-working class shortlists. Could we, perhaps, have all-Pakistani shortlists for seats such as Hodge Hill and Sparkbrook?

A CHRISTIAN WELCOME—THEN AND NOW!

"Washing one's hands of the conflict between the powerful and the powerless means to side with the powerful, not to be neutral"—Paulo Freire[148]

It is important to mention that, during those early days of multiracial Birmingham, some sections of the city community were more welcoming of immigrants and responded to their needs. According to Sutcliffe & Smith (p365), the Christian churches were one such group. "In March 1950 the Birmingham protestant churches jointly set up a Coordinating Committee for Overseas National." According to Prem, it was the first city to take such a step. In the same year, a resolution was passed at the diocesan conference calling attention to the Christian duty of caring for the well-being of newcomers. Two years later "the Archdeacon of Birmingham went to see the Lord Mayor, Alderman Bowen, about the problems of coloured people and the matter was submitted to the General Purposes Committee." The Coordinating Committee later came to be the Birmingham Community Relations Council. Some of the Christian leaders were also active in race equality at the national level. A number of the early Christian projects aimed at ethnic minorities are to be found in 'Faith in the city of Birmingham', published in 1988; many more innovative organisations have come into being since then. On another occasion, it was reported that in Birmingham cathedral, a lone bell had tolled at midnight on 28 February 1968. Pulling the bell was Bishop Sinker, Provost of Birmingham, and inside the Cathedral an hour-long vigil was held in sorrow at Britain's broken promises to the Kenyan Asians.

During my time in Birmingham, I have observed the growing contribution of Christian projects and organisations in this respect. Even more of them are active now. Taj's comments on the Christian church in Bradford apply equally to Birmingham. He referred to their commitment and active role in "promoting good inter-communal relationships and in speaking out on behalf of the poor and disadvantaged." He had acknowledged their "considerable presence in the area, at a significant cost, with valuable effect. They deserve recognition from the wider community for their genuine goodwill and the positive effect of their efforts."

For me, one of the most radical documents that came from the national Christian community was 'Faith in the City'[149], published some thirty years ago. In my view what it said (para 12.45) about ethnic minorities in general is still true for Pakistani-Birmingham so I have paraphrased it accordingly:

> *Decisive policies and programmes are required at city level to eliminate racism, both personal and institutional, and to establish a society in which the presence of Pakistanis is affirmed. Such policies and programmes have to be made effective across Birmingham, especially within neighbourhoods.*

> *There is a need for many more Pakistani—focused community organisations to address the problems of racism in their areas, becoming more alert not only to what is being done but also to what is left undone. A statement of anti-racist intent would be the starting point to ensure that important questions are not overlooked.*

> *Is the Pakistani community kept informed? Are their needs and priorities discussed and understood in the right places? Do the mainly White organisations discriminate, consciously or unconsciously, against Pakistanis or do they stand solidly alongside them when they are oppressed? Are there positive anti-racist attitudes in local youth clubs and community centres, especially in parts of Birmingham where Pakistanis are a minority? Are the names of Pakistanis put forward for key decision-making bodies?*

All religions provide a bonding and 'networking' opportunity for their members. The challenge for Christians is whether this is used to further their existing advantages or to promote justice for the excluded. Dr Toby Howarth, now the Secretary for Interreligious Affairs for the Archbishop of Canterbury and who has spent many years in Birmingham has pointed out[150], with particular reference to Luke's gospel, that Christians should not be 'tribal' i.e. just there for themselves. Instead, they should be there for the others.

It is said there are three different types of social capital: bonding, bridging and linking[151]. The Pakistani community is fine on the first. I have discussed the second under cohesion. As for the third, I believe the 'broker' role of Christians referred to in paragraph 5.55 of the 'Faith in the City' is still relevant within the Birmingham context. There is much still to be achieved and where the Christian church can play a critical role for the foreseeable future. As the 'establishment' organisation, it continues to have privileged access to power which it can use for the benefit of the current 'other', the Pakistanis. It has been pointed out that all religions provide a 'networking' opportunity for their members[152]. The challenge for Christians is whether this is used to further their existing advantages or to promote justice for the excluded.

IN CONCLUSION

In homage to a fellow Pakistani, Sarfraz Manzoor, who was talking about what England, meant to him, for me Birmingham is very special. It has been my home; not just since 1970 but going back to the 1950s when my father came here and others from our family and community helped to regenerate the city. They sweated in the local factories and foundries, in conditions and at rates of pay which were unacceptable to the local population and living in overcrowded houses which had been abandoned by the indigenous population.

The city is where I have received the best of my education. Having begun life sitting on the dusty floor of my primary school and later the bench of my secondary school, I have been able to access the best education on offer, with more to come as I near the completion of my PhD. Where else would that have been possible but here, in this land of opportunity.

It was here that I fell in love with music and literature and later love of a different kind. Birmingham is personal. I care very much what happens to the city. It has become a success which needs to continue. The Pakistani community and the city are intertwined. If the community prospers so will the city. The opposite is not worth contemplating. Over a hundred years ago, W.E.B. DuBois, the American civil rights activist pointed out that the challenge of the twentieth century was to find a solution to the problem of the 'colour line'. For me, the challenge we face, here in Birmingham, is to make sure that the Pakistanis in the city are able to succeed.

In writing this note, my aim has not been to demonise Whites or more generally the non-Pakistanis who between them run the city but to raise everyone's awareness of what is happening around us;

about the tsunami that is coming our way. I have tried to identify the collective processes across the city which may be responsible for failing and excluding the Pakistanis in the hope that people will come off the fence and stop taking a 'nothing to do with me' attitude. To quote Paulo Freire; to be neutral in a battle between the powerful and the powerless is to take sides with the powerful. I also wanted to give a wakeup call to the Pakistani community who may at times have colluded with their own exclusion but now need to struggle for a different future for the sake of forthcoming generations.

It has been pointed out that liberalism generally favours sameness over difference[153]. But, this may not be a question of either/or but more a continuum. Thus, the closer a group is to liberal ways, the more preferred it is and, conversely, the more different a group, the less likely it is preferred. There are said to be "limits on the degree of difference" liberals will tolerate, even talk of "too much difference" and "some differences as needing to be excluded, marginalised", leading to the really different not being tolerated, even despised.

In the same way, liberals and the organisations they run have often taken a blanket approach to equality. But, this often fails to recognise the differences between groups and their particular historical trajectories and unequal access to power. Furthermore, it ends up privileging some groups (some ethnic minorities, even some Asians) over others.

Such an approach, based on the assumption of prior sameness, has, in Birmingham, disadvantaged the Pakistani community. They were behind others to begin with and have remained so, with some exceptions. A local teacher I spoke to, who has some understanding of history, pointed out that Pakistani disadvantage goes back to the days of the Raj when Indian Muslims were at the bottom of the pile.

We seem to have reached a point where we like to think that we are meritocratic, that is, we are fair towards everyone, we are tolerant of people's race and religion, we have a neutral liberal elite and our universal services reach everyone equally. In my view little of this is true when it comes to Pakistani-Birmingham. Equality is a myth, especially if one looks at 'equality of outcome'.

According to Bhikhu Parekh, racial inequality exists when a group is treated unequally because of its race. "Its members might be subjected to systematic discrimination in employment, education, criminal justice system . . . . Or they might suffer from severe material disadvantages caused by present or past acts of ill treatment and enjoy unequal access to the basic conditions of the good life. Or they might be stigmatised, subjected to demeaning stereotypes, treated as an inferior species and socially avoided." [154.] It takes little to figure out how this may apply to Pakistani-Birmingham.

Although, I am clear of the problem, I am less certain as to the cause of the problem or indeed what we can do about it. I will, nevertheless, offer a comment on the situation and make suggestions for a possible response in the hope that others will similarly offer their solutions.

A TIME FOR LEADERSHIP, AGAIN!

For Bhikhu Parekh "every generation enters the flow of history at a particular point in time and inherits a past with its painful and pleasant memories. Although it cannot undo the past and disown the burden of painful memories, it can lighten their weight by undoing at least some of the effects of past injustices and cruelty. In doing so, it civilises the past, reduces its moral burden, redeems the honour and good name of its forebears and bequeaths to succeeding generations a better past and a less fractious society."[155] It is within our control to 'civilise' the past and help shape a different future for our city.

There is a tradition of others looking to our city for leadership. People like our 'Lunar Men' led the rest of the country by their own example of courage and innovation. In race relations we have also been seen as leaders by others with similar communities and needs. For example, our 'English for Immigrant pupils', under the leadership of Mr Chapman, was seen, during the 1960s, as an exemplar by the government. We continue to be seen "nationally as a leading authority in the field of race equality" and what we do has "significance beyond the city itself."[156]

For our city to become a truly multi-ethnic, multi-cultural, vibrant, 21st century city would send a most powerful message to the rest of Britain (and Europe). "What happens in Birmingham will impact on the ways in which other towns and cities engage with their diverse populations. It is of unparalleled importance, then, that we succeed in this endeavour."[157]

To go back to that comment from Sir Albert Bore (Evening Mail, 3 May 2000), referred to above, I would say that, to achieve such a position, it is important to recognise that 'diversity' and 'harmony' are not mere adjectives; to exploit their fullest potential for our community it is necessary to approach them more strategically.

The Lawrence Commission had said:

> *"It will require strong leadership if the racism we have encountered is to be addressed. This will entail the open acknowledgement of institutional racism within organisations and the explicit identification of action to combat it."*

> *"The time has come for Birmingham's civic and political leadership to be imaginative in the field of race equality, as it is in other aspects of the city's life."*

The above Commission had gone onto recommend the setting up of a Birmingham Academy of Excellence to provide "a large group of first class, skilled and talented minority ethnic managers. Birmingham has the opportunity to set an example and to achieve a national and international reputation in this field." I would suggest that such an initiative is set up specifically for the Pakistani community.

In 1967, C. West Churchman came up with the concept of 'wicked problem'—not wicked in the sense of being evil but because of its complexity and lack of obvious solutions. Horst Rittel and Melvin M. Webber then formally described the concept in 1973.

'Wicked problems' are said to be socially complex, have multiple causes and interdependencies and are said to have resulted from chronic policy failure. They hardly ever sit in any one's area of responsibility so they get neglected. Everyone can say: 'it's not my problem or we will leave it to someone else'. The problems often, if not always, lack clear solutions. Even when a solution is found, it usually requires a change to behaviours and challenge to orthodoxies.

We seem to have our very own 'wicked problem' as outlined above. For a response, I would like to conclude with the words of Professor Michael Clarke at Birmingham University, which he had offered in the introduction to the 'Good City';

> *"None can wish anything other for Birmingham than that we find a creative way of informing and helping fashion the debate about what the city should be, where it should be trying to go and the nature of "community" within it. If we are to achieve this, then we must be prepared to take the proverbial "blank sheet of paper", challenge assumptions and conventions and cast aside the temptation to say "but it can't be done."*

SECTION 4

POSITIVE ACTION FOR PAKISTANIS

"What we are saying is that from now on, regardless of other considerations, 20 per cent of recruiting must come from ethnic minorities. We are going to monitor recruitment and managers will have to explain if they have not recruited 20 per cent. It is no good just talking of being committed to an equal opportunities process—we have to demonstrate that we mean what we say." Bill Gray

"The institutions should take steps to ensure that they address the current under-representation of minority ethnic people in their employment. All institutions should establish workforce targets based on the current minority ethnic population of the city . . . You can performance manage so many things, why can't you performance manage race?" Lawrence Commission

In the past, we have had in Birmingham, at least within education where I worked, the attitude: 'we are Birmingham; we are different'. Whatever came down from the central government, we used to adapt it before putting it into practice. We had the stature and the confidence to change national policy to suit our particular situation. Of course, the time I am referring to, we were led by that giant of education leaders, Professor Sir Tim Brighouse. Reading *The Lunar Men*, one certainly gets the impression that our founding fathers, the Matthew Boultons, the James Watts . . . . were giants of their times. I am sure we still have courageous leadership which can stand upto central government and others.

All are not the same

It was Yogi Berra who famously said 'If you don't know where you're going, how are you gonna' know when you get there?' In the same way we need to work out where we are going as a city. What does our future look like? By the time (Pakistani) Muslims are a majority in our city, who will be doing what jobs and at what grades and what services will we be providing and how? Will the Pakistanis be active participants in the process or passive recipients?

We have to ask ourselves as a city community what kind of equality we want. Is it one that treats everyone the same; where jobs and services are made available, leaving it to chance as to who benefits. Or we look at the data to decide who is benefitting from such opportunities, which group of people less so than others and decide a different approach. So we start with the results or the outcome in mind and work backwards. We could decide on the numbers of Pakistanis to be employed in the city from the chief officer downwards and then set out to achieve that result.

During my recent time with the Council we operated what was described as the Logic Model to design services. It has resulted from the work of Paul McCawley at Idaho University 1997[158]. The model could be used to shape our wider city future.

The model has the following components:

- *Outcomes* to be achieved i.e. a fair and just Birmingham society for all including Pakistanis
- *Activities* to achieve the outcomes are then worked out i.e. employment opportunities are made available free of anti-Pakistani discrimination and services are offered which are appropriate for Pakistani needs and circumstances
- *Investment* to make it happen is made so there is ring-fenced funding from existing mainstream budgets as well as additional funding being allocated

DWP 360 pointed out the following:

- Pakistanis had low levels of education and qualifications, low levels of confidence, limited experience of different types of jobs, and limited networks of contacts in different sectors.

- Employers making assumptions about the way a Pakistani employee in some public facing roles (for example, a solicitor) would relate to the White community, and this, despite the efforts of individuals, confining their opportunities to working within ethnic minority organisations
- Graduates driving taxis and waiting at tables . . . (leading to people thinking that) gaining a graduate qualification does not necessarily translate into moving into a better job
- Some graduates lacking any experience of work, particularly women who may not have been allowed to work by their families whilst studying. "This is in contrast to other students who may have worked Saturday jobs . . . . and who may have worked evenings and weekends whilst at university"

Equality does not mean 'sameness'

We seem to be surrounded with a universal approach to provision of services. Could this explain health and education inequalities? Birmingham has certainly done very well in raising the overall education standards. Ever since the days of Professor Sir Tim Brighouse, we have come be an authority that sets its own high standards and improves against our previous best. As a result, each year, we do better than before and better than the other 'like' authorities. Of course, while we have made tremendous progress overall, with the Pakistanis also improving compared to their prior situation, the gap between them and the other groups has got bigger because the others have improved at a faster rate.

There is sufficient evidence to show that treating everyone the same does not always work given people have different starting points. In his autobiography, *Who goes home,* Roy Hattersley pointed out that treating all ethnic minorities as if they were the same was a form of unintentional racism.

In education, we talk of 'differentiated' approach. We do it in mixed ability classes where children are treated differently. We do it even more in teaching special needs students—smaller classes, longer time, greater resources. In the world of sales and marketing, they call it 'segmenting'. So different potential customers are treated differently. Each day we have phone calls from some Urdu speaking person who tries to approach us as a long lost relative and tries to sell us something. They have decided, purely based on our name, on what approach to take with us. I don't think for a minute that they do the same with people who are called Smith or Jones. In the world of equalities, it is called 'equality of treatment (according to need).

> *"It is very well making policy pronouncements, but you have to take it much further than this. It is just not enough to have fine pieces of paper . . . In employment, for example, you need to take a whole view . . . . If you recruit ten black people and ten years later they are in the same position, that's not equality"* Black Officer (Solomos and Back)

Also within equalities, the term Positive Action, can be a way of taking targeted action in response to particular needs. Under Section 11 of the Local Government Act 1966, funding was provided to local authorities to help meet the 'special and additional' needs of ethnic minorities in schools. However, Positive Action continues to be one of the most misunderstood terms. People think it means positive *discrimination*, which, of course is illegal. The employer, Amey, above had assumed that the term went against the merit principle.

The earlier rules about Positive Action—in place since the Sex Discrimination Act 1975 and the Race Relations Act 1976—have now been changed. In the past, it was limited to training or encouragement such as mentoring schemes for ethnic minority or women staff where they were under-represented at certain levels within an organisation or needed additional training provision. At Bilston Community College, we had used the legislation to put into place programmes such as 'Women into Management', 'Women into Construction' and 'Black Access into Teaching'.

Under the recent Equality Act 2010, it is now legal to recruit or promote a candidate (say a Pakistani) who is of equal merit to another candidate. However, before this can be done the employer has to reasonably think that Pakistanis are under-represented in the workforce and they suffer from a disadvantage due to being a Pakistani. For example, a service for teenagers has no employees who are Pakistani, despite being located in an area of high Pakistani population. When a vacancy arises, there are two candidates who are equally qualified for the job and the employer has to find a way to choose one of them. One candidate is Pakistani and the other candidate is not. Under the current law, it would be legal to offer the job to the Pakistani and the other candidate would not be able to make a claim of unlawful racial discrimination.

In my view, the new Positive Action rules offer us as a city a way forward. However, I would not suggest that a few organisations take such an approach in isolation from each other. Thinking of our city as one big business, Birmingham Plc, which is faced with across-the-board Pakistani under-representation, I would like to propose a wholesale programme of Positive Action, properly resourced and co-ordinated and with one clear focus: to improve the situation for Pakistanis in employment and service provision. A number of organisations speak of 'reflective workforce'. I am suggesting that the words should be put into practice as far as Pakistani-Birmingham is concerned.

According to a government report (DWP 406) [159] charting the practice from a number of countries, Positive Action measures can include providing cultural and religious awareness training amongst employers and workforce monitoring.

In the USA one of the most effective instruments for promoting positive action in employment is contract compliance by the government as a purchaser of goods and services. This is where public authorities specify certain social criteria that a contractor who wants to obtain government contracts must meet.

But, according to the above report, introduction of a similar programme in the UK would require the production of more detailed statistical data which is currently not available. It was pointed out that "many employers in the UK, even those 'chosen as leaders in equal opportunities policies' do not have effective workforce monitoring to even a basic level." The National College, a government agency, appears to be one such employer which lacks appropriate data on its sub-contracting organisations.

Good practice examples from the past

Solomos and Back pointed out that Birmingham has been very successful with regard to writing policies and presenting an image of itself as an authority that is in the forefront of developing race equality policies. However, it has not been as good at making sure that race equality initiatives are embraced at all levels within the organisation. The authors quote a Black officer saying: "We have created a façade that race relations have been strengthened. We go all around Europe, host conferences blowing Birmingham's trumpet but the reality of the situation is very different . . ." (p191)

But, it would appear that it is not all window-dressing. There is much good practice from the past that we can learn from. I thought this Birmingham political leader, quoted in Solomos and Back summed up my thinking on positive action as it relates to the Pakistani community:

> ". . . . If you have a history of under-representation you've got to do something at some point to catch up, but I am against the dropping of standards. I think what you've got to do is remove any other and illegitimate obstacles, personal racism of a superior within a department or something of that sort, overt discrimination. Remove that so that people can compete fairly. What I wouldn't do is remove competition."

As a policy response for the Pakistani community, we could do worse than refer to the 1984 manifesto commitment of Birmingham Labour Party. As pointed out in Solomos and Back, it committed the incoming administration to seek to achieve "proportionate employment of ethnic minorities . . . at all levels." It committed the Council to take Positive Action to ensure that there is equality of opportunity for ethnic minorities in all its initiatives. As a result, the City Council successfully pursued a target of twenty per cent ethnic minority employees, under the leadership of Bill Gray who is quoted above.

Following this, there was writing of equal opportunities criteria into the performance contracts of senior managers. The Chief Officers of service departments made regular reports to the Personnel and Equal opportunities Committee (though this resulted in some "embarrassed and heated exchanges with members, it worked"). The "situation had been transformed radically." By 1993, the ethnic minority presence in the City's workforce had reached 15.4%, with a "number of departments approaching the target 20 per cent minority employment and some have completely transformed their ethnic composition."

I am simply suggesting that we do for the Pakistanis now what we did then for ethnic minorities in general. I am sure we have a few Bill Grays who could offer similar leadership to marshall support across the city's employers and service organisations.

It is necessary to point out that Positive Action is step one. If it doesn't work then positive discrimination, of the kind Trevor Phillips has talked of below, may have to be resorted to.

EQUAL TREATMENT IN SERVICES ACCORDING TO (NOT IRRESPECTIVE OF) NEED

"Reflective workforces are seen as effective workforces and if you are going to provide culturally competent and sensitive services then you need staff who can connect with the communities that they serve"—BRAP

"Being customer-driven requires acute sensitivity and empathy with the needs and aspirations of all our citizens"—Bruce Gill

Commenting on the early welfare system, the feminist writer Fiona Williams described it as 'false universalism'. She pointed to a bias in favour of male workers; in a context where the concept 'breadwinner' meant a man. Could a similar process be happening now in Birmingham of 2012 where services are not exactly universal for the Pakistani community? Could it be that the services carry the biases of those who design and deliver them? We know very few of them are Pakistanis. Does this mean that Pakistani perspectives are not taken into account within these services? According to Atkin "service users . . . are assumed to have Western attitudes, priorities, expectations and values; act according to Western ways; speak English and understand the organisation of public services." While for Bhikhu Parekh, "in the absence of an explicit recognition of others' cultural differences, we are constantly tempted to understand and judge them on terms of the categories of our own culture, and thus to assimilate them to our ways of thought. While appearing to treat them equally, we end up treating them unequally."[160] Based on the concept of women-friendly services could we aim for 'Pak-Aware' or 'Pak-Friendly' services?

Here is an illustration of how the universal or 'open door' approach to service provision is operated and how it ends up discriminating, albeit unintentionally, against the Pakistanis. I shall explain with reference to a school, a funding organisation, the library service and the Pakistani community.

I was in a Birmingham secondary school which in the past couple of years has come to have a majority Pakistani population. The senior staff member I was talking to told me their students did not read enough at home and that this was impacting on their exam results. Clearly, the school were expecting pupils to read at home. It is not clear whether they had done anything about it to encourage this practice. Did the Pakistani parents know that this was something their children should be doing? Had anyone told them about this? Possibly not, because it is likely to be assumed that everyone knows that reading for pleasure is important in the learning process and can help a young person achieve better results. Except, the 'everyone' in reality means middle class people who have been through the education system, possibly upto and including at university level.

It just happened that my next meeting was at the offices of the Arts Council, where I was to meet the officer with responsibility for promotion of literature. As an aside, I had met the officer at a writers' conference in Digbeth. It was organised by Writing West Midlands for all writers in the area but it only attracted a mainly White audience. Out of over one hundred and fifty people, there were probably less than ten Black and Asian faces, a couple of us from the Pakistani community. Events like these provide a good opportunity for writers to meet others like them as well as publishers and bodies such as the BBC. We know there are many Pakistani writers in Birmingham. I am sure it would be possible for the Arts Council and Writing West Midlands working in partnership with the local Urdu Writers or Urdu promotion societies to bring Pakistani writers to an event. Of course, to reach this particular destination, the journey might have to be planned differently.

At my meeting with the Arts Council, I asked what initiatives had the Arts Council targeted at the Pakistani community to encourage their take-up of literature. The officers pointed out that they did not target their work at particular communities. "The organisations we fund are based in Birmingham. Because Birmingham is a diverse community, we believe such an approach would reach diverse users." In other words, a universal, approach was taken with an open-door policy. Whoever saw fit to take-up whatever was offered would receive the benefit. If there are people in the community, such as the Pakistanis, who may not realise the importance of literature for their children's education, then that is their own fault. The Arts Council and the organisations and projects it was funding were not responsible!

Could the schools work in partnership with the libraries, community groups, parents and the Arts Council to come up with a way to encourage reading amongst Pakistani young people? I am sure none of it is rocket science. Until then the outcome will remain as it is. Young Pakistanis and their parents will go on not knowing that reading at home is beneficial for education and not taking advantage of much that is out there funded by bodies such as the Arts Council. And the Pakistani writers will go on not benefiting from services offered by Writing West Midlands. They and groups such as the BBC and the publishing community will go on not knowing each other. Then the next time the BBC want to put on a play that has Urdu content, it will not have any idea where to begin or the Urdu writer who has written such a play and wishes for it to be given airtime she will not know who to contact. So, it could be a win-win. The trouble is none of these organisations have decided to exclude the Pakistani community. They are open to all who wish to take advantage of what is on offer. It's your tough luck if you do not. No one is going to come chasing you. If you don't take up the services, it will just mean there is more for others. Land of opportunity Birmingham maybe but until services reach the people who need them and according to their needs, there is little benefit. This is a point as much for the service providers as it is for the Pakistani community.

> *"If public services are to be effective in responding to more diverse needs, then a pre-requisite is to ensure that their workforce profiles are truly reflective of (the) diversity."* Lawrence Commission

26 Library Faces; none from Pakistani-Birmingham

The other people who are critical to reading and literature for young people are the Birmingham Library Service. By chance, I came across a little news item in a culture magazine, one of those free ones you can pick up from a number of city outlets. It was saying they were looking for people to apply to become 'Faces' of the new library. Given my long-term connection with Birmingham Library Service, starting at Bloombsbury Library, I thought I would apply. I also told them in my application that I work in schools as a writer with mainly Pakistanis students who I encourage to read more and join their local library. I also told them how I had given my time for free to help start the cataloguing of the Mahmood Hashmi Collection at Birmingham Archives. (The job was later completed by Councillor Abdul Rashid, ex-Lord Mayor of Birmingham.)

Sadly, my application was not successful. I was provided a full explanation as to why my face was not the right one for them:

> *Your application clearly showed that you are a true advocate for libraries and indeed have actively contributed in a voluntary capacity at Central Library. However we have received a great many applications from people telling us, as you did, about their love of reading and enthusiasm for libraries. The people we have chosen for our next group of faces . . . have more distinctive stories to tell about the impact of libraries on their lives . . .*
>
> *With best wishes*[161]

At the time they had only recruited half of the 'Faces'. I began to monitor the situation to see whether they select any Pakistanis. They have now finished their recruitment. Sadly, it would appear that none of the 26 Faces is from Birmingham's 153000-strong Pakistani community.

In early welfare provision, which was aimed at everyone, the concept of means-testing was to acknowledge that people had different needs and circumstances. What is the equivalent needs analysis for Pakistanis in service provision? Is there any under-representation amongst the users? Is it across the city? Or just in certain areas and communities? In any case, is it simply a case of equal access i.e. anyone who wants to is more than welcome to benefit from the service on offer? Or should we aspire to achieve equality of take-up or equality of outcome? This would require us to monitor who is benefiting from services and who is not. We would then be able to take remedial action. The Faces for the new library were recruited in phases. Surely, it could have been seen during the recruitment process that no Pakistanis had been accepted (maybe no one applied other than me). Then something could have been done about the situation.

This way we would not be in the situation we are in where none of the 26 faces are from the Pakistani community.

As well as arguing for equal treatment according to need, instead of irrespective of need, I believe we also need to explore the relevance of inverse proportions i.e. greater the need, greater the resource allocation. So, if schools think Pakistani pupils have a greater need to read then more resources will need to be allocated to this.

When I was asked to produce biographies of 20 Birmingham Asians, I decided to have some sense of proportionality. So the resulting group contained, as intended, Pakistanis, Indians, and Bangladeshis in proportion to their presence in Birmingham. I tried to equally divide the group between men and women and young and old. Could the Library Service have taken a similar approach and aimed for ten percent of the faces to be from the Pakistani community (based on overall population) or possibly twenty five percent (based on Pakistanis in schools)

Nearly a decade ago, Sir John Bourn, Head of the National Audit Office had said that for public services to meet their full potential they had to respond to the needs of our diverse society. They had surveyed 131 government bodies and produced a report which said that knowledge of diverse needs of customers, diversity of the workforce and the success in providing effective services tended to go hand in hand. Sir John had gone onto say that tailoring public services was a way of achieving efficiency and effectiveness and "making sure they actually benefit all those they are designed to serve."[162]

In my view the Lawrence Commission perfectly sums up what is needed:

> "In other words, if public services are to be effective in responding to more diverse needs, then a pre-requisite is to ensure that their workforce profiles are truly reflective of this diversity . . ."

Meanwhile is it fair to assume that the sensitivity and empathy referred to by the then Acting Head of Equalities Bruce Gill[163] is not possible for Pakistanis service users, given few of them are actually employed in the delivery of such services? More generally, does it mean that in the light of un-reflective workforces, we do not have effective workforces? Does this also mean that Birmingham service providers are not in a position to provide a culturally competent service?

How can some of the Birmingham service organisations claim to be 'fit for purpose' if they do not have the benefit of a Pakistani perspective? What sort of health, crime or education service will be delivered if it has not had such a perspective, gained first-hand? A non-Pakistani going on a course or reading a book to learn it is not the same.

The Lawrence Commission pointed out that "public service institutions should explicitly embrace the reality of the changing demographic profile of the city and take active steps to ensure that services are planned, arranged and delivered to be responsive to a more ethnically and cultural diverse population."

During the British Raj, they had a group of employees who were called *interpreters*. These were White people—the Orientalists—who had close knowledge of the Indians and who helped to act as a 'bridge' between the rulers and the subjects. I am suggesting that we employ Pakistanis to do a similar job in Birmingham's many organisations. However, it is critical that, just as they did in India, the employees concerned are rewarded for their knowledge and expertise. It's ok to occasionally have to explain to a colleague what Eid means or engage in small talk about the origins of balti food. This is part and parcel of workplace relationships. But, when one is forever on-call as *cultural expert*[164] or as a linguistic interpreter, then it is only right and proper to have one's efforts recognised like any other area of expertise. Furthermore, such staff will also, from time to time, need opportunities for continuing professional development.

Data in the 1970s told us what was coming our way in terms of the ethnic makeup of our city. The predictions have come true. And yet the service and employment systems, with some exceptions, go on behaving as if the world in Birmingham is all-White, where universal services are all that is needed. My worry is that if we don't wake up to the situation we are facing, it will actually become worse. The tsunami will be upon us and take us all down.

In 2006, Trevor Phillips, the then head of the Equality and Human Rights Commission thought it may be time to bring in 'positive discrimination'[165]. His comments were made in relation to the serious levels of under-representation of Muslims within the police service. He had said that the service was not 'fit for purpose'. I believe this to be the case for a range of service areas and organisations which have few or no Pakistanis. As an example of how the new system might work, Mr Phillips cited the Police Service of Northern Ireland, where the law was changed to allow it to recruit half of all its new officers from the Catholic community. Elsewhere, Mr Phillips had supported positive discrimination in favour of young Whites.[166] After many years of researching educational underachievement, I also made a similar recommendation for the White working class.[167]

Culturally competent services

> *"All services are culturally competent and able to work with service users from the Pakistani community"*—Birmingham East and North Primary Care Trust

Phillimore from Birmingham University has pointed out that "the job of ensuring effective service provision for all has never been harder, with basic information lacking about who is out there, what their needs are, and how those needs might be met." (WTWM) It may be hard but it is not an insurmountable task, as shown by the above quote from Birmingham East and North Primary Care Trust who appear to have already achieved what is needed. The Trust has within its catchment area, the majority of Birmingham's Pakistani community (106000 out of 153000). Their comment was made in reply to my Freedom of Information request. It would be worth finding out the details from them so one could offer this as a model of good practice. I would also like to suggest two resources in this respect. The first is the one I produced for the then Department for Children, Schools and Families[168] while the second one outlines what is meant by cultural competence[169].

Speaking of health services generally, it has been pointed out that many professionals "often lack appropriate and necessary knowledge about the South Asian families they have contact with and do not understand how to adapt services to meet their cultural and religious values." They speak of "highly qualified yet ignorant professionals" and say "the education they have received has proved inadequate to the situation they are faced with. It is inexcusable because the population change has not happened overnight." [170]

There is a misguided belief amongst many of our secular practitioners that it is possible to separate what people do, who they are, their 'worldly' needs from their religion and culture. For the Pakistani community religion and culture are often inseparable; what they do and who they are is intertwined with their beliefs and values. Their 'worlds' can be more integrated than for many others in our community. In my view, therefore, in the New Birmingham, it is necessary to replace 'regardless of . . .' with 'due regard to . . .' in employment and provision of services. Religion and culture need to be integral to the 'story' rather than be an extra who is given a walk-on part as an afterthought.

I am not in a position to comment as to the extent of cultural incompetence in our services, other than to say we do not have an alternative and not just for Pakistanis. This is even more critical where it concerns sensitive areas of need.

Pro-active Services

There is often a tendency to design services and then fit the users to them. I believe, instead we should start with the needs of the (Pakistani) user and design appropriate services and then aim to deliver them in a culturally competent manner.

At the time of writing, Ramadan (or Ramzaan), the month of fasting had just finished. Eid-ul-Fitr had been and gone. This was to be followed up by Eid-ul-Zua, (also known as Eid-ul-Adha). Each year, across our city, at this time there are men and women preparing to go on the Hajj pilgrimage to Mecca. Not surprisingly given our size of the local Muslim community, there are many of them.

Every year I read in the Urdu press (the mainstream English newspapers like the Birmingham Mail are rarely interested in such things, though, arguably they should be) of some incidents which the hajjis have to face. Sometime, there are life and death matters. Whenever I read the news, I wonder whether we could make things better for the travellers and send with them a team of Hajj Support Workers from Birmingham. We could have a small regular team for the city, employed throughout the year. This could be supplemented at Hajj time with short-term workers and volunteers. These could be Muslims drawn from across the city's employers. This could form part of corporate social responsibility; just as giving staff time off for such activities as Territorial Army. I am sure together they could make things better for the hajjis. Just imagine the goodwill it could generate within the Muslim community. It would certainly be a way to say to the Muslim community: 'thank you for making your home in our city; here is a little token of our appreciation for what you have done for Birmingham'.

I came across some data which reported that people within the Pakistani community spent 50 or more hours as unpaid informal carers[171].

Some of this will be focussed on a relatively new phenomena for our society; that of 'Elder-Care' in the home. I wonder how the city's services are shaping up to look after the Pakistani elders as an increasing number need someone other than their family to look after them in the latter years, as well as to give their families, mainly women, a much deserved break.

Justice for Pakistanis

> *"The time has long passed where we need separate* (equality) *units, they have served their purpose and it has got the issues on the agenda. We don't want marginalised units, they can't be effective because they can never really implement initiatives. These issues have to be at the core of things. I want to see more than commitment . . . . How do you measure commitment? You can only measure commitment by what is achieved"*—Solomos and Back

Birmingham City Council has a critical and strategic role in this respect. But they are not the only ones. We must not forget the Police and the National, the world standard universities, Health Service organisations—Strategic Health Authority, the hospitals—who are very large bodies indeed with millions of pounds in their budget. If they are in Birmingham and are designed to serve the people of Birmingham then they should equally be expected to provide justice for Pakistanis. They should have the fullest understanding of the community's needs and have a properly funded strategy to meet those needs.

Unlike Mr Jinnah, I am not asking for such justice to be achieved through separatism but the exact opposite. I am suggesting that Pakistanis be fully integrated into the life of the city which they currently are not.

When outsiders come in and take a look at our city, they often go away with a very positive picture. Similarly, when we speak to external bodies, it is very easy to talk, in glowing terms, about our diversity. But, looked at closely, the situation is a little different. We continue to practice identical double-speak when it comes to equality, especially in relation to Pakistanis. It is nothing short of 'theoretical equality' with sentiments of 'not too many please'.

Frederick Douglas was a famous Abolitionist. In 1872, he was nominated as the vice presidential candidate on the Equal Rights Party ticket with Victoria Woodhull, the first woman to run for President of the United States. He was said to be a firm believer in equality of all people, whether black, woman, Native American, or recent immigrant. He pointed out that power concedes nothing without a demand. It never did and it never will. "Find out just what any people will quietly submit to and you have found out the exact measure of injustice and wrong which will be imposed upon them, and these will continue till they are resisted . . . ." There is much here for us to reflect on!

A ROUTE MAP FOR THE JOURNEY AHEAD; THE BIRMINGHAM PRINCIPLES

"The case of Northern Ireland and positive action on religious equality in employment may also be particularly pertinent for Britain at a time when many Muslims, Sikhs and others complain of religious discrimination, when the most disadvantaged groups in the labour market are Muslims . . ."—Department of Work and Pensions

I would like to suggest that we look back to the 1980s and the work of two Church of England bishops; Bishop Wood and Bishop Shepherd. The former was Wilfred Wood whose first job was as a priest in St Paul's Cathedral in 1962. After fulfilling a number of roles, he was consecrated as Bishop of Croydon in 1985. He was a champion for racial justice. His 'Wood Proposals' had contributed to the setting up of the Community Relations Commission, the forerunner for the Commission for Racial Equality.

David Sheppard was the Bishop of Liverpool who played cricket for Sussex and England. His book, 'Bias to the Poor', had a radical message; not just about equality but justice. In it, he stated very clearly the principles which underpin positive action:

"Some whole groups find themselves shut out from the circles in which decisions are taken and where many opportunities exist. Does God not have a word for those who have advantages? He does indeed have a word for all men; it is not always the same word. 'Where a man has been given much, much will be expected of him.

Sometimes His word to the advantaged is that they must surrender
their advantage for the sake of the poor"

Between them, the two Bishops came up with the Wood-Shepherd Principles[172]. In India, they have something similar with the aim of promoting equality for the Dalit community formerly known as 'untouchables'. Theirs were known as the Ambedkar Principles[173], after their leader, Bhimrao Ramji Ambedkar.

Here, it is also worth mentioning the Northern Ireland Fair Employment legislation whose focus is on the promotion of equity for Catholics. According to DWP 406 "the introduction of proactive equality instruments accompanied by the political will to bring about social change can have a significant impact on employment equity."

I see the principles as a route map or after the sculpture by Clark Fitzgerald in Coventry Cathedral, as a 'plumb line' for the city.

While, in drafting these principles, I have operated within our current legal framework, it may be necessary in the future for new laws to be passed to facilitate what we wish to do in the unique situation that is Birmingham.

The Birmingham Principles

General

1. We believe that discrimination against Pakistanis is unacceptable and we will do everything possible to eliminate it
2. We believe that our workforce should, at all levels and grades, reflect the Birmingham community in relation to its Pakistani makeup
3. We as a community, especially the elite of Birmingham, recognise the need to re-educate ourselves and review our worldview. To do so, we propose to adopt Edward Said's Orientalism as a guiding text for the City.
4. We will take a differentiated approach to addressing inequalities.

Employers

5. We will operate within the full requirements of the West Midlands Common Standard for Equalities in Public Procurement

6. We will allocate board and senior management responsibility to make sure the equality policy is implemented and regularly reviewed as necessary

7. We will use fair and transparent recruitment, selection and career development processes, avoiding word-of-mouth methods and commit to clear objective criteria, and ensure that these processes are open to scrutiny

8. We will create an ethos of understanding and respect in relation to culture and religion and monitor the religious composition of the workforce

9. We will take full responsibility for our workforce, both direct and sub-contracted, including in the supply chain, by seeking to detect and remedy any form of discrimination against Pakistanis and Muslims of Birmingham

10. We will, with immediate effect, set out to achieve a 10% Pakistani presence in the workforce and then sign up to 'Target 20: 20', that is, 20% of Pakistani employees by 2020.

11. In all our education institution we will set and monitor targets for recruiting, training, retaining and promoting Pakistani teachers in proportion to their students

12. We will develop and implement a plan of Positive Action appropriate to our organisational context. This will aim to address underrepresentation of Pakistanis, including of Pakistani women

13. We will take any pre-recruitment steps necessary to increase the skill level of Pakistani job applicants

14. We will review all personnel specifications and the concept of 'merit' in order to take account of the large Pakistani presence in the city

15. We will consider accepting 'Pakistani' as a 'Genuine Occupational Qualification'

16. We will have an effective system in place to help with reporting of employees' complaints and grievances

17. We will review the composition of the workforce and employment practices every three years (based on the Northern Irish model) to ensure that the Pakistani community enjoys fair participation in employment

Equality of service provision

18. We will undertake a full assessment of the needs of the Pakistani community, including its sub-sections e.g. young, women, elderly

19. We will remove all barriers in service provision for the Pakistani community, including the physical and practical; social; cultural and linguistic and religious.

20. We will vigorously monitor the take-up of (especially universal) services, analyse poor take-up and 'recalibrate' the services and how they are offered.

21. We will capacity-build Pakistani groups and organisations and work with them in developing outreach services

22. We will review our 'ways of working' so that services and professionals take account of the religious and cultural context of the Pakistani community.

23. We will aim for a culturally and religiously competent workforce that reflects the Pakistani presence amongst the users and the city, whichever is greater. We will also aim to be responsive to other religions and cultures present in the city.

24. We will employ teams of 'experts' within all service areas who can advise on the needs of the Pakistani community.

25. We will pay attention to language needs of the users and make sure we have sufficient staff who are able to communicate in Urdu and the dialects used within the Pakistani community

26. We will undertake regular surveys in order to receive feedback from Pakistani users and then review our services accordingly

Procurement

27. We will make sure that all employers and service providers who are in a contractual relationship with the Council fulfill their fullest commitment on equalities as laid out in the Equalities Standard.

28. We will favour 'Pakistani-equal' companies when awarding contracts

29. We will make sure there is transparency in the recruitment of consultants through open advertising. We will also monitor the ethnicity of the consultants we employ and regularly report on the results.

Education

30. We will put in place an anti-racist multicultural 'Birmingham Curriculum' which will focus on our community's history from the Lunar Men to the present day, including the study of the British Raj, the Indian contribution to the World Wars and the development of our post-war diverse population.
31. We will provide an updated guidance for all schools on the cultural and religious needs of Pakistani and Muslim pupils
32. We will encourage "twinning" between schools in different parts of the city to enable the sharing of information and learning from one another.
33. We will look to the government for changes in education law so that Academies and Free Schools conform to local authority framework on religious education and actively support and promote the SACRE work and resources.

Governance

34. We will make sure, with immediate effect, that all governing bodies and boards (e.g. schools, colleges, universities, Health Trusts) reflect the Pakistani presence in their user constituency

Arts, culture and media

35. We will make sure that Pakistanis are a part of the city's picture including all press and media and arts and culture organisations
36. We will make sure that accurate and balanced information is provided on all cultures and religions present in the city, especially the Pakistanis and Muslims. We will make good use of our libraries and other information outlets in this respect.
37. We will put in place a 'rebuttal' unit which provides immediate response to negative and inaccurate portrayal of the Pakistani community

Food and drink

38. Our city centre restaurants will provide halal food as a part of their normal menu provision and we will review our alcohol-based economy in order to reduce the exclusion of Muslims.
39. We will fully comply with Food Standards Agency guidance[174] and instruct all our officers to routinely inspect the validity of halal food claims and take action against businesses which mis-describe products

Pakistani Awareness

40. (In order to help create the pre-conditions for equality) We will put in place a programme across the city to enable the whole of the Birmingham community to develop an appreciation of Pakistani culture, the history of the community in the city as well as the wider aspects of Islamic contribution to civilisation
41. (Based on advice from the Department of Work and Pensions) We will, for our current employees, embark on a city-wide training programme of awareness of religion, especially Islam.
42. We will build into all job descriptions and person specifications the requirement for such understanding amongst new employees.

Cohesion

43. We will instigate a 'One Birmingham' programme to bring our communities together, building on the achievements of pilot projects such as Near Neighbours and The Feast
44. We will learn from the work of the post-Apartheid Truth and Reconciliation Commission and President Clinton's 'One America' project and instigate similar dialogue initiatives for Birmingham

Research

45. We will undertake research, develop practices and pilot innovative ways of working on matters of importance to Pakistani-Birmingham. This will include the 'social evils' of

Islamophobia and racism especially that which is targeted at the Pakistani community within Birmingham

46. We will raise our levels of understanding about our unique situation, learning from the examples of others (such as Malaysia, Ireland, South Africa and India) who have Positive Action schemes in place for both minorities and majorities.

47. We will undertake research on 'positive discrimination' measures (in the unlikely event that Positive Action does not work)

48. We will commission research on the potential role of religion for the 'Good Birmingham' as a part of our strategy to bring it into the mainstream

Audit

49. We will develop a city-wide team of **independent** Community Auditors whose job will be to undertake audits of employers and service providers against the Birmingham Principles

50. We will publish an annual progress report on implementing the Birmingham Principles and be open to answer questions on policies and practices from organizations and the general public.

AND FINALLY, DEAR BIRMINGHAM

When I began this project, I had a general idea, or what academics call a thesis, about Pakistanis in Birmingham. This was that the community was marginalised and lived a parallel life to the rest of the city. At that time I had little evidence, with the exception of education.

The Pakistani Network had made a number of statements about the 'Pakistani-Birmingham problem'. I can only agree with them. By chance, I recently discovered a website which provides people an opportunity to write a 'Dear Birmingham' letter "in order to share something with Birmingham . . . (to) educate, enlighten, inform, challenge . . ."[175] I hope I have done that with my letter. They suggest "short and punchy" letters; maximum 250 words. It was on 14 March 2011 that I had emailed my MP and arranged to see him at his surgery in Sparkbrook. I have taken all that time, and a few more words, to elaborate on the statement by the Pakistani Network, that the "rapidly increasing population of Pakistani heritage residents has major social and political implications for Birmingham:

- The future economic success of Birmingham is directly linked to the success of its Pakistani heritage population, especially young people.
- The city needs to evolve its political and administrative structures to reflect the needs of this growing population.
- The Pakistani heritage residents need to move into non-traditional areas to improve community cohesion and integration into the mainstream life of the city.
- The community needs to break its insular mentality and build strategic partnerships with other communities to develop a shared and mutually supportive vision for the city."

To use a residential metaphor, the Home that was built by the Lunar Men has served us well. However, it needs some modifications in order to make it fit-for-purpose for the foreseeable future. Like the Lawrence Commission, I hope Dear Birmingham will "contribute to securing real improvements" in this respect, not just for Pakistani-Birmingham but for the whole city.

When I started writing this social commentary, I had in mind a document which I thought could be a model for my work. This was "A Black Manifesto 2005." Its most recent edition has been produced by the 1990 Trust with support from some forty Black and race equality organisations.[176]

I had thought then that maybe my document could similarly be called 'A Birmingham-Pakistani Manifesto' but now I believe that this is a mainstream agenda for the whole city, for all organisations and peoples who live or work here and who only want the best for My Hometown.

Please join in the conversation

As I began to gather statistics and other information, I was sure that any day now someone would come along and prove me wrong. They would give me information—on their Pakistani service users, Pakistani staff and Pakistanis on their governing body or board—which proves my thesis wrong. It would say quite clearly and categorically:

> "*Karamat Iqbal, you are WRONG. Our organisation is not like that. We have it all sorted. Our workforce reflects the Pakistani presence in Birmingham. And they are not all employed at the bottom grades. Our general staff are culturally competent and are able to properly and appropriately meet the needs of the Pakistani service users. And we have the right percentage of Pakistanis in our governing or decision-making body.*"

But not a single Birmingham organisation came back with such a response. Every reply I had to my request for information, convinced me that I was right in what I believed to be the case. Wherever I looked, I have found evidence of what the Lawrence Commission described as "a 'dual city'—a city doing well on the one hand, which is predominantly white and middle class, and a city doing badly on the other, which is overwhelmingly made up of (Pakistani) communities who are socially excluded and geographically segregated in deprived neighbourhoods." This was one situation where it would have actually pleased me to be proved wrong.

But it's not too late. Please join in the conversation with me.

If there is someone out there who thinks I am wrong about Pakistani exclusion, about the failure of our organisations, our employers, our service providers, then please contact me to tell me so. Of course, you can also write in and let me know if I have got it right!

One suggestion made while I was writing this was that I should include some examples of good practice. While I have not been able to do so on this occasion, with your help, I would like to publish an update of Dear Birmingham. So please send me any examples of work with the Pakistani community which you would like to share with others.

I can be contacted at *karamat@forwardpartnership.org.uk*

Thank you

Karamat Iqbal

ANNEX 1

Pakistanis in Birmingham 2005 (estimated City Council data)

Washwood Heath	72%
Springfield	65%
Bordesley Green	62%
Sparkbrook	54%
Hodge Hill	49%
Nechells	33%
Lozells & E. Handsworth	33%
Hall Green	32%
Moseley & Kings Heath	31%
Aston	28%
Soho	28%
South Yardley	28%
Acocks Green	23%
Stechford & Yardley Nth	21%
Handsworth Wood	14%
Edgbaston	12%
Billesley	11%
Selly Oak	10%

ANNEX 2

% of Birmingham pupils achieving 5+ A*-C by ethnic group and gender 2006-2011

Ethnic group	2006	2007	2008	2009	2010	2011
B. Cbbn boys	24	26	27	33	39	45
B. Cbbn girls	37	35	49	48	50	56
White boys	40	39	41	46	51	55
White girls	47	47	51	51	58	61
B/deshi boys	36	34	38	44	52	63
B/deshi girls	40	40	53	49	63	61
Indian boys	57	60	69	68	68	76
Indian girls	65	67	71	73	81	86
Pak boys	29	33	35	37	47	50
Pak girls	35	39	45	48	57	58
All boys	37	38	40	44	50	55
All girls	45	46	51	52	59	61

ANNEX 3

PAKISTANI PRESENCE IN EDUCATIONAL INSTITUTIONS

King Edward Foundation schools and Academies

School	Pakistani pupils %	Pakistani staff %	Pakistani governors Numbers
King Edward VI Handsworth School	12	1.2	
King Edward VI Camp Hill School for Boys,	12.8	1.25	0
King Edward VI Camp Hill School for Girls	14.2	0.08	0
North Birmingham Academy	15	1.9	*
Shenley Academy	1.58	0	*
Heartlands Academy	34	13	*

Colleges of further education

College	Pakistani students %	Pakistani staff %	Pakistani governors Numbers
Birmingham Metropolitan College	15	2.26	1 (this is a student)
Bournville College	3.56	1.7	1
City & South Birmingham College	23	5	4 (out of 19)
Joseph Chamberlain Sixth Form College	51	11.8	2
Sandwell College	13	2.21	0
Solihull College	6.8	2.62	0
The Sixth Form College, Solihull	14	1	1
Cadbury Sixth Form College	20	17	1
Fircroft College of Adult Education	4 (Access) 2.7 (short courses)	1	1

Universities and colleges of higher education

University	Pakistani students %	Pakistani staff %	Pakistani governors numbers
Birmingham City University	7	1.86	Ethnicity not recorded
University of Wolverhampton	5.9	0.47	0
University College Birmingham	7.2 (FE); 11.6 (HE)	1.4	0
Newman University College	7.5	1	1
Birmingham University	2.74	1.2	
Aston University	8.3	2	

ANNEX 4

COMMON STANDARD FOR EQUALITIES IN PUBLIC PROCUREMENT

Level 1 (5 to 49 employees)
1. All firms with more than five employees must provide a written racial equality policy (or general equalities) policy which covers at least: (a) recruitment, selection, training, promotion, discipline and dismissal, (b) victimisation, discrimination and harassment, making it clear that these are disciplinary offences within the firm (c) identification of the senior position with responsibility for the policy and its effective implementation, and (d) communication of the policy to staff.
2. Effective implementation of the policy in the firm's recruitment practices, to include open recruitment methods such as the use of job centres, careers service or press advertisements.
3. Regular reviews of the policy.
4. Regular monitoring of the number of job applicants from different ethnic groups.

Level 2 (50 to 249 employees)
5. Written instructions to managers and supervisors on racial equality in recruitment, selection, training, promotion, discipline and dismissal of staff. These can be instructions for general equal opportunities in employment.
6. Training in racial equality for managers and any staff responsible for recruitment and selection. This may be in the form of general equal opportunities training.

7. Monitoring of (a) the numbers of job applicants for employment from different ethnic groups (b) the numbers of employees from different ethnic groups, by grade and section.

8. If monitoring reveals under-representation of particular ethnic groups, action to check that criteria 1-3, & 6-7 are being used effectively in the firm, and to make changes if necessary.

Level 3 (250 or more employees)

9. Regular consultation on racial equality issues within the workforce.

10. Regular ethnic monitoring of selection, transfer, training, promotion, discipline and dismissal.

11. Mention in the firm's recruitment advertisements and publicity literature of its arrangements for offering equal opportunities, including racial equality.

12. If monitoring (as in criteria 7 and 10) indicates under-representation of any group, take action to (a) check that criteria 1-3, 5, 6, 9 and 11 are being used effectively within the firm (b) take advice about appropriate action from officers from the CRE, Racial Equality Councils or the Race Relations Employment Advisory Service, all of whom offer free advice, and (c) take appropriate action (including positive action) as a result of that advice.

ANNEX 5

Other suppliers to the City Council

During November 2012, the City Council made the following payments, roughly calculated. Accurate data can be found on *http://www. birmingham.gov.uk/payment-data*. The names are just a few from a very long list. The key questions are whether these suppliers comply with the requirements of the Equalities Standard and the number of Pakistanis they employ.

	£
• Aggregate Industries Ltd	247,000
• Altodigital UK Ltd	108,000
• Anchor Trust	127,000
• Atkins Ltd	133,000
• Barnard0's	210,000
• Birmingham Rep	124,000
• British Cycling Federation	138,000
• British Gas	(the list of payments ran over 7 pages)
• Bromford Corintha Housing Assoc	144,000
• BUPA Care Services	173,000
• Capita	(the list of payments ran over 6 pages)
• Centro	78,000
• Chinbrook Family and Community	109,000
• Community Solutions	781,000
• Corona Energy	(the list of payments ran 8 pages)

- EDF Energy   (the list of payments ran 3 pages)
- Extra personnel   (the list of payments ran over 8 pages)

- FCH   168,000
- Foster Care Associates   332,000
- Galliford Try   915,000
- Geofrey Osborne Ltd   121,000
- Glendale Managed services   287,000
- Global Property   114,000
- Haystoun Construction   235,000
- Ideal Fostering   137,000
- Jessup Brothers   152,000
- Keepmoat Homes   617,000
- Kids   125,000
- Kier Partnership Homes   656,000
- Mears ltd   2380,000
- Morrison Facilities   533,000
- NSL Ltd   265,000
- PH Jones   559,000
- Quadron Services   509,000
- Royal Mail Group   398,000
- Serco Ltd   339,000

REFERENCES

[1] *http://www.guardian.co.uk/uk/2004/nov/21/race.pakistan* downloaded 08 03 2013

[2] The Nation (Urdu newspaper) 1-7 March 2013: 'We need to create a distance between our young people and sectarianism and extremism'

[3] *All equal—but not all equal to us http://www.guardian.co.uk/books/2013/mar/27/why-left-wrong-mass-immigration* Downloaded 13 04 2013

[4] Muslims in Birmingham, Tahir Abbas, *http://www.compas.ox.ac.uk/fileadmin/files/Publications/Research_projects/Urban_change_settlement/Muslims_community_cohesion/Birmingham%20Background%20Paper%200206.pdf* downloaded 26 02 2013

[5] *https://www.birminghambeheard.org.uk/consultationDetail.aspx?consultationid=1177* downloaded 08 03 2013

[6] A guide to getting involved in Birmingham, *http://www.birminghambeinvolved.org.uk/media/1159/Be%20Involved%20Booklet.pdf* downloaded 08 03 2013

[7] *http://www.pcdn.co.uk/articals.htm* downloaded 16 4 2012

[8] Geoff Mungham and Geoff Pearson (1976): Working class youth culture

[9] John Rex and Robert Moore (1967): Race, community and conflict

[10] Muhammed Anwar (1979): The myth of return

[11] White disadvantaged pupils in Birmingham *http://www.publications.parliament.uk/pa/cm200809/cmhansrd/cm090519/halltext/90519h0011.htm* downloaded 06 03 2013

[12] A man's a man, a study of colour bar in Birmingham and an answer *http://www.search.connectinghistories.org.uk/engine/resource/exhibition/standard/default.asp?resource=1180* downloaded 31 01 2013

[13] Philip N Jones (1976): Colored Minorities in Birmingham, England, Association of American Geographers vol 66 no 1

14 Martin A Plant (1971): 'The Attitudes of Coloured Immigrants in Two Areas of Birmingham to the Concept of Dispersal, Race & Class 12: 323

15 Ian Stephens (1964): Pakistan

16 Peter Fryer: Staying Power, 1984, p381

17 A Sivanandan (1982): A different hunger

18 Kevin Searle(2013): 'Mixing the unmixables' the 1949 Causeway Green 'riots' in Birmingham Race & Class, 54:44

19 Mike Phillips & Trevor Phillips 'Windrush: the irresistible rise of multi-racial Britain' 1998, page 198

20 Times Educational Supplement 'Hope has to be the new Black' 16 October 2008

21 Arthur Schlesinger(1993): The disuniting of America

22 Birmingham Stephen Lawrence Inquiry Report: Council response *http://www.lgcplus.com/lgc-news/birmingham-stephen-lawrence-inquiry-report-council-response/1348215.article* downloaded 25 01 2013

23 Barriers to employment for Pakistanis and Bangladeshis in Britain *http://research.dwp.gov.uk/asd/asd5/rports2005-2006/rrep360.pdf* downloaded 31 01 2013

24 *http://www.youngfoundation.org/files/images/Cities_in_Transition_-_FINAL.pdf*

25 *http://www.birminghameconomy.org.uk/sum/kfsumempeth.htm* downloaded 29 12 11

26 Delivering on diversity' Black Workers' Group Conference 2001

27 Birmingham City Council, Budget 2013 *http://www.birmingham.gov.uk/budgetviews* downloaded 05 03 2013

28 The Birmingham Post Comment: Cultural diversity needs more than talk *http://www.thefreelibrary.com/The+Birmingham+Post+Comment%3A+Cultural+diversity+needs+more+than+talk.-a0114389210* downloaded 31 01 2013

29 Birmingham City Council, Equality and Diversity *http://www.birmingham.gov.uk/jobs-eo* downloaded 25 01 2013

30 Racism and Recruitment 1986

31 City Council: Report to the Children and Education Overview and scrutiny Committee, 22 04 2009' (p2)

32 LA schools data, *http://services.bgfl.org/cfpages/newperform/compleas.cfm?phase=5&group_id=24*

33 Recruitment and retention strategy for primary and secondary school teachers in Birmingham 2007-2012

34 Commissioned, in 2001, by East Birmingham *Plus* Parents Association

35 *http://www.services.bgfl.org/myportal/custom/files_uploaded/uploaded_resources/2150/Equality_report_v1.pdf* downloaded 31012013

36 University of Birmingham, Dr Ranjit Sondhi, BSc, OBE *http://www.birmingham.ac.uk/council/membership/ranjit-sondhi.aspx* downloaded 31 01 2013

37 The position of women and BME staff in professorial roles in UK HEIs *http://www.ucu.org.uk/media/pdf/9/6/The_position_of_women_and_BME_staff_in_professorial_roles_in_UK_HEIs.pdf* downloaded 20 02 2013

38 Gifted and talented education—the case for inclusion *http://www.teachingexpertise.com/e-bulletins/gifted-and-talented-education-case-inclusion-7708* downloaded 09 03 2013

39 GC Spivak: Can the subaltern speak? *http://www.maldura.unipd.it/dllags/docentianglo/materiali_oboe_lm/2581_001.pdf* downloaded 31 01 2013

40 Birmingham Centre for Contemporary Cultural Studies (1982): Empire strikes back

41 Fathers and family centres *http://www.jrf.org.uk/sites/files/jrf/1859353118.pdf* downloaded 14 03 2013

42 Tracking the Decision-making of High Achieving Higher Education Applicants *http://www.suttontrust.com/research/tracking-the-decision-making-of-high-achieving-applicants/* downloaded 14 03 2013

43 Astonishing figures on the £12bn problem facing the NHS *http://www.itv.com/news/2012-09-10/whats-the-biggest-problem-facing-the-nhs/* downloaded 31012013

44 *http://www.publications.parliament.uk/pa/cm200809/cmselect/cmhealth/286/286.pdf* downloaded 31012013

45 *http://www.humancity.org.uk/reports/publications/UNEQUAL%20LIVES%20-%20OCTOBER%202010%20-%20WITH%20COVERS.pdf* downloaded 25 01 2013

46 *http://www.patient.co.uk/doctor/Ethnic-Matters.htm* downloaded 31012013

47 *http://www.Blackradley.com/wp-content/uploads/2012/02/TheyMovedLikeFishReport.pdf* downloaded 31013

48 Summary report on Islamophobia *http://fra.europa.eu/sites/default/files/fra_uploads/199-Synthesis-report_en.pdf* downloaded 31 01 2013

49 Interim workforce equality monitoring report 2012 *http://www.uhb.nhs.uk/Downloads/pdf/EdMonitoringReport.pdf*

50 How to define our diverse city? ; White plight (on White educational underachievement); White working class; a case for Positive Action?

51 State of the third sector 2011-2012

52   Email: 7.9.2011

53   Email 13.9.2011

54   'Working for an inclusive Britain' Michael Orton And Peter Ratcliffe

55   Email 22.9.2011, Lynda Aspley, Corporate Procurement Services

56   *http://www.marketingbirmingham.com/about_us/company_structure/the_ board/* downloaded 04 02 2013

57   *http://en.wikipedia.org/wiki/Cultural_imperialism* downloaded 04 02 2013

58   Religion in England and Wales: findings from the 2001 Home Office Citizenship Survey

      http://www.dharmapeople.com/ftp/SACRE_RE/RE_SURVEY_2001_452454. pdf downloaded 04 03 2013

59   'An analysis of race equality policy and practice in the city of Birmingham UK' Local Govt Studies vol 31, no 1, 53-68

60   *http://www.birminghamfuture.co.uk/content/leading-campaigner-talks-divercity* downloaded 11 10 2012

61   *http://fairbrum.wordpress.com/*

62   Birmingham Business Charter for Social Responsibility *http://www. finditinbirmingham.com/Upload/Tom%202/BBCSR%20final%20draft.pdf* downloaded 02 02 2013

63   The Nation (Urdu newspaper) 19.06.2004.

64   Marta Bolognani (2007): Community perceptions of moral education as a response to crime by young Pakistani males in Bradford, Journal of Moral Education Vol. 36, No. 3, September 2007, pp. 357-369

65   *http://bmorereadinggroup.files.wordpress.com/2012/04/ebooksclub-org__the_ racial_contract.pdf* downloaded 26 01 2013

66   The Opinions of Mirpuri Parents in Saltley, Birmingham, About Their Children's Schooling *http://www2.warwick.ac.uk/fac/soc/crer/research/ publications/miscpub/reprintp_no.2.pdf* downloaded 26 01 2013

67   Birmingham Multicultural Support Service, Winter/ Spring 1988

68   Reporting diversity: How journalists can contribute to community cohesion *http://www.societyofeditors.co.uk/userfiles/file/Reporting%20Diversity.pdf* downloaded 23 02 2013

69   Henri Nickles et al (2010): A comparative study of the representations of "suspect" communities in multi-ethnic Britain and their impact on Irish communities and Muslim communities-mapping newspaper content

70   Birmingham: Where The World Meets, 05 February 2013 (hereinafter referred to as WTWM)

71   *http://www.economist.com/node/170771* downloaded 31 01 2013

72 *http://www.guardian.co.uk/society/2005/nov/30/equality.guardiansociety supplement* downloaded 31 01 2013

73 CRE Employment Report 3 August 1981

74 Albert Memmi: Racism 2000

75 John Dovidio: The subtlety of racism, Training and Development April 1993

76 Justice and the politics of difference,1990

77 Bob Hepple & Erika Szyszczak (1992): A case for positive discrimination in Discrimination; the limits of the law: Bob Hepple & Erika Szyszczak (ed)

78 *http://www.guardian.co.uk/books/2000/jul/08/society* downloaded 01 02 2013

79 The banality of evil, *http://www.informationclearinghouse.info/article7278.htm* downloaded 01 02 2013

80 *http://www.publications.parliament.uk/pa/cm200809/cmselect/cmhaff/427/42703.htm* downloaded 11 03 2013

81 Aversive racism and selection of decisions, *http://www.stanford.edu/group/scspi/_media/pdf/Reference%20Media/Dovidio_Gaertner_2000_Discrimination.pdf* downloaded 11 03 2013

82 Critical race theory and education, *http://eprints.ioe.ac.uk/1661/1/Gillborn2006critical11.pdf* downloaded 31 01 2013

83 *http://www.youtube.com/watch?v=8G16urFgo5s*

84 'The racialised somatic norm and the senior civil service' (2001), Sociology 35: 651

85 Akbar Ahmed (1997): Jinnah, Pakistan and Islamic identity

86 Niall Ferguson (2003): Empire, p349

87 *http://www.thefreelibrary.com/13+arrested+in+National+Front+protest.-a075632797* downloaded 07 03 2013

88 White flight, Prospect February 2013

89 Richard Wilkinson & Kate Pickett (2009): The Spirit Level

90 Talja Blokland (2003): Ethnic complexity; routes to discriminatory repertoires in an inner-city neighbourhood, Ethnic and Racial Studies Vol. 26 No. 1 pp 1-24

91 Raymond Williams (1968): Resources of Hope

92 *http://www.thefeast.org.uk/about/what-we-do/* downloaded 06 03 2013

93 *http://www.muslimnews.co.uk/paper/index.php?article=6120* downloaded 14 03 2013

94 *http://www.cuf.org.uk/near-neighbours/about* downloaded 06 03 2013

95 John Dixon and colleagues (2010): A Paradox of Integration? Interracial Contact, Prejudice Reduction and Perceptions of Racial, Journal of Social Issues, Vol. 66, No. 2

96   One America in the 21st century, *https://www.ncjrs.gov/pdffiles/173431.pdf* downloaded 25 01 2013

97   The dignity of difference- how to avoid the clash of civilizations 2003

98   Forgiveness in our Faith Traditions—Birmingham *http://www.uk.upf. org/index.php?option=com_content&view=article&id=382:forgiveness-and-reconciliation-birmingham&catid=38:community-cohesion&Itemid=109* downloaded 10 03 2013

99   Truth and reconciliation of South Africa report *http://www.justice.gov.za/trc/report/finalreport/Volume5.pdf* downloaded 04 02 2013

100 Tania Tam and colleagues (2008): Postconflict Reconciliation: Intergroup Forgiveness and Implicit Biases in Northern Ireland, Journal of Social Issues, Vol. 64, No. 2

101 Anthony King (1991): Culture, Globalisation and the World-System (p56)

102 Tariq Modood (1994): Political Blackness and British Asians, Sociology 28: 859

103 John Rex (1991): Ethnic identity and ethnic mobilisation in Britain

104 Three steps to power, *http://www.chamberlainforum.org/?p=1749* downloaded 31 01 2013

105 *http://web.warwick.ac.uk/fac/soc/CRER_RC/publications/pdfs/Research%20 Papers%20in%20Ethnic%20Relations/RP%20No.%204%20(checked).pdf* downloaded 26 01 2013

106 BRAP 2002

107 Eduardo Bonilla- Silva (1997): Rethinking racism: towards a structural interpretation, American Sociological Review vol 62, no 3 465-480

108 Mark Tunick (2006): Tolerant imperialism: John Stuart Mill's defence of British rule in India, The Review of Politics vol 68, no 4

109 *http://www2.lse.ac.uk/newsAndMedia/news/archives/2012/08/ FromPardesiToDesi.pdf* downloaded 26 01 2013

110 *http://www.jrf.org.uk/system/files/1861348223.pdf* downloaded 31 01 2013

111 Change and Continuity Among Minority Communities in Britain *http://cep. lse.ac.uk/pubs/download/dp0903.pdf* downloaded 31 01 2013

112 *http://www.jrf.org.uk/system/files/1861348223.pdf* downloaded 20 02 2013

113 An Exploration of the Teenage Parenting Experiences of Black and Minority Ethnic Young People in England *https://www.education.gov.uk/publications/ eOrderingDownload/RW41.pdf* downloaded 04 02 2013

114 Mark Halstead (1997): Muslims and Sex Education, Journal of Moral Education vol 26, no 3

115 Modood and others (1994): Changing ethnic identities PSI

116 James Arthur et al: 'The values and character dispositions of 14-16 year olds in the Hodge Hill Constituency

117 *http://www2.warwick.ac.uk/fac/soc/crer/research/publications/miscpub/reprintp_ no.2.pdf* downloaded 04 03 2013

118 *http://www.faithsforthecity.org.uk/more_events.html*

119 What makes a 'Good City'?*http://www.faithsforthecity.org.uk/Papers/Sikhism. pdf* downloaded 26 01 2013

120 After 7/7: Sleepwalking to segregation *http://www.humanities.manchester.ac.uk/socialchange/research/social-change/ summer-workshops/documents/sleepwalking.pdf* downloaded 31 01 2013

121 *http://www.newstatesman.com/politics/politics/2012/05/halal-hysteria* downloaded 26 01 203

122 *http://image.guardian.co.uk/sys-files/Guardian/documents/2001/12/11/ communitycohesionreport.pdf* downloaded 26 01 2013

123 Valentine and others (2010): Contemporary cultures of abstinence and the nighttime economy: Muslim attitudes towards alcohol and the implications for social cohesion, Environment and Planning A 42: 8-22

124 Drinkjing places *http://www.jrf.org.uk/sites/files/jrf/2113-where-people-drink. pdf* downloaded 31 01 2013

125 That's what she said *http://www.nus.org.uk/Global/Campaigns/That's%20 what%20she%20said%20full%20report%20Final%20web.pdf* downloaded 14 04 2013

126 *http://www.ed.ac.uk/polopoly_fs/1.82423!/fileManager/Triq%20Modood.pdf* downloaded 26 01 2013

127 Safeguarding in Faith- 28 April 2012

128 Religion and the role of the school, The Swann Report *http://www. educationengland.org.uk/documents/swann/swann08.html* downloaded 06 03 2013

129 'The Fourth R'. The Durham Report on Religious education. Report of an independent commission set up by the Church of England Board of Education and the National Society for Promoting Religious Education. 1970.

130 Dialogue and Conflict on Religion. Studies of Classroom Interaction in European Countries *http://www.e-cademic.de/data/ebooks/extracts/ 9783830922728.pdf* downloaded 26 01 2013

131 *http://www.Blackradley.com/wp-content/uploads/2012/02/TheyMoved LikeFishReport.pdf* downloaded 26 01 2013

132 Revised guidelines on meeting the religious and cultural needs of Muslim pupils *http://www.bgfl.org/bgfl/custom/files_uploaded/uploaded_ resources/11129/MuslimGuidelines.rtf* downloaded 15 03 2013

133 Schools for Muslims (2001), Oxford Review of Education vol 27, No 4, 515-527

134 Daniele Joly (1995) Britannia's Crescent: making a place for Muslims in British society

135 Information downloaded 18 September 2012 from the City Council website under 'Commitment to equality of opportunity: Teaching in Birmingham

136 *http://www.jrf.org.uk/publications/experiencing-ethnicity-discrimination-and-service-provision* downloaded 03 02 2013

137 Ghazala Mir and Aziz Sheikh (2010), in Ethnicity and Health, vol 15, no 4 327-342

138 Faith in the city, Dr Chris Allen *http://www.birmingham.ac.uk/research/impact/perspective/faith-allen.aspx* downloaded 23 02 2013

139 *http://www.dharmapeople.com/ftp/SACRE_RE/RE_SURVEY_2001_452454.pdf* downloaded 03 03 2013

140 'Religion as cuckoo or crucible' Journal of Moral Education v 35, No. 4, December 2006, pp. 571-594

141 *http://www.birminghammail.co.uk/news/local-news/vandals-attack-bournville-college-building-161465* downloaded 31 01 2013

142 *https://www.ncjrs.gov/pdffiles/173431.pdf* downloaded 31 01 2013

143 Alastair Bonnett (2000): White identities

144 *https://pantherfile.uwm.edu/gjay/www/Whiteness/Underst_White_Priv.pdf* downloaded 31012013

145 *http://www.timwise.org/*

146 *http://dadyal.com.pk/there-is-more-to-me-than-my-competence-in-english/* downloaded 01 02 2013

147 *http://i-epistemology.net/attachments/847_Ajiss21-3%20-%20Abbas%20-%20After%209%20over%2011.pdf* downloaded 26 01 2013

148 The Politics of Education: Culture, Power, Liberation, (1921, p122)

149 Faith in the City- a call for action by Church and Nation 1985

150 *http://hmd.org.uk/resources/podcasts/dr-toby-howarth-secretary-for-interreligious-affairs-for-the-archbishop-of-canterbury* downloaded 17 1 2013

151 Robert D Putnam: Bowling Alone 2000

152 Robert D Putnam & David E Campbell: American Grace 2010

153 Irene Gedalof ()2013: Sameness and difference in government equality talk, Ethnic and Racial Studies vol 36 no 1 117-135

154 Achieving racial equality (2005) in Loury G and others (ed): Ethnicity, social mobility and public policy

155 A case for positive discrimination (1992) in Discrimination; the limits of the law: Bob Hepple & Erika Szyszczak

156 Race equality and education in Birmingham *http://www.bgfl.org/custom/files_uploaded/uploaded_resources/10398/gillborn-report.pdf* (p ii) downloaded 31 01 13

157 BRAP 2002: Beyond racial identity, p62

158 *http://www.uiweb.uidaho.edu/extension/LogicModel.pdf* downloaded 02 02 2013

159 Developing positive action policies: learning from the experiences of Europe and North America *http://research.dwp.gov.uk/asd/asd5/rports2005-2006/rrep406.pdf* downloaded 02 02 2013

160 Achieving racial equality (2005) in Loury G and others (ed): Ethnicity, social mobility and public policy

161 Email 4.10.2011, Sara Rowell, Client Project Manager, Library of Birmingham

162 *http://www.personneltoday.com/articles/15/12/2004/27169/nao-report-warns-public-services-must-respond-to-diverse.htm* downloaded 07 03 2013

163 Delivering on diversity—Black workers' group conference report

164 Tehmina Basit and Ninetta Santoro (2011): Playing the role of 'cultural expert': teachers of ethnic difference in Britain and Australia, Oxford Review of Education vol 37 no 1

165 *http://www.dailymail.co.uk/news/article-391255/Legalise-positive-discrimination-sake-national-security.html* downloaded 26 01 2013

166 *http://www.telegraph.co.uk/news/uknews/3270989/Trevor-Phillips-calls-for-positive-discrimination-to-help-young-Whites.html* downloaded 26 01 2013

167 *http://www.tes.co.uk/article.aspx?storycode=6061775* downloaded 31 01 2013

168 *http://forwardpartnership.fcw-service.com/wp-content/uploads/sites/7/2011/11/equality-and-diversity-issues-in-family-intervention-services.pdf* downloaded 02 02 2013

169 *http://www.socialworkers.org/practice/standards/NASWCulturalStandards.pdf* downloaded 02 02 2013

170 Ghazala Mir and Phillip Tovey (2002: Cultural competency: professional action and South Asian carers, Journal of Management in Medicine 16, 1

171 *http://www.1990trust.org.uk/system/files/bm_2010_full.pdf* downloaded 14 03 2013

172 *http://www.methodist.org.uk/index.cfm?fuseaction=opentoworld.content&cmid=2284* downloaded 01 10 2011

173 *http://idsn.org/fileadmin/user_folder/pdf/New_files/IDSN/Ambedkar_Principles_brochure.pdf* downloaded 05 02 2013

[174] Guidance note on halal food issues, 29. 09. 2010, ENF/E/10/0 *http://www.food.gov.uk/multimedia/pdfs/enforcement/enfe10038.pdf* downloaded 14 04 2013

[175] *http://dearbirmingham.com/#!/about* downloaded 09 03 2013

[176] The black manifesto, *http://www.1990trust.org.uk/black-manifesto* downloaded 14 03 2013

Lightning Source UK Ltd.
Milton Keynes UK
UKOW041827050513

210210UK00001B/22/P